THE FASTING CHRONICLE :

GROWING FROM MILK 2 MEAT

Peter "Gospel Professor" Eley

THE FASTING CHRONICLE:

Growing from Milk 2 MEAT

Peter "Gospel Professor" Eley

DEDICATION

This book is dedicated to my wife Felicia Eley for her loyal unwavering support in all of my endeavors. You are the best, honey.

Acknowledgements

I would like to acknowledge my Savior Jesus Christ; He is the reason why I live. I would like to recognize my Facebook family for all of your encouragement and support while I was on the fast and the writing of this book. I would also like to give thanks to my dear friend Pastor Charlie Biggurs for all of the inspirational text messages that you sent on a daily basis that kept me going. I would like to also acknowledge my church family www.Christtemplechurch.com and my many family members and friends. Lastly, I would like to express special thanks to my editor Georgina Chong-You and John Widener my technical guru. You all are the best!

Foreword

BoldFace

By: Dorothy "aW" Williams

You thought you were **BOLD** when you stepped up to the
Lord

Now look at you

You got knocked down

Quick as lighting He flicked you out of heaven and
smushed you in the ground

NOW

You a fallen angelic being

You're disgusting to me like green string beans

Which Means

I can pick up and detect your tricks and schemes

And I'm callin them by name

You Slanderer, Tempter, Deceiver

You are a Liar, a Disguiser, a Falsifier

You just plain sick

Foreword

And I'm sick...

And tired of all your attacks

The Body of Christ is no longer sittin' back!

And I know we made our mistakes, but don't get it twisted, we no longer associates

I'm standing on the Lord side having a good time being confident and courageous

Fanatically audacious!

And I recognize you as my adversary, but I have an advocate

I'm on duty Beelzebub and I ain't gon quit

But I'm a lean wit it, rock wit it, be **BOLD** and crunk wit it!

I'm sorry your many names are suppose to move what? Who?

Brother please, I got names too

I'm more than a conqueror

I'm a child of the King

Yea Go 'head and get scared I got the Lord in my ring

Foreword

And He's your most dangerous predator, your biggest competitor

Foreva eight, nine, ten steps ahead

Cuz we Wise like that

We Rise like that

And know that we don't ever run from you, but we run at you cuz we **BOLD** like that

And I 'am need you to remember that

And since you don't, go 'head and sit there so I can smack your memory back

As I flip through the pages and take you back to the days of old

READ

In Exodus chapter 7 through 11

How Moses was **BOLD** when he said 'Let My People Go!'

And Esther was **BOLD** when she said, 'King if it be pleasing…'

And David was **BOLD** when he said,

'You can come at me with you spear and sword, but I come at you in the name of the Lord!'

Foreword

So see Satan, this is evidence that we don't have to take
this

But with God's strength we **BoldFace** this

And through it all, I'll still be a persuader with Paul and all
y'all

That nothing will ever separate me from the Love of God

Now get out there and do a work for God

Put on His whole armor

Make sure that feet's shod

With the preparation of the Gospel of Peace

No matter where you go, you reach souls and tear up
Satan's lease

And tighten up that belt of truth buckled around your waist

And hang that breastplate of righteousness right in place

I'm a lover of hats, but this one's my favorite

When the enemy tried to mess with my head it saved my
life

It's called the Helmet of Salvation

So throw down that fear and grab hold of your Faith

Foreword

It's a shield, a force field promised to protect and keep ya
safe from all the enemy's slap, kicks, punches and blows

And any demon that attempts to touch or come close will
ignite then explode!

And my weapon is loaded

Cha chic, Say hello to My little friend

It's the Word of God and it sealed your fate and tells your
end

Nope, you're not a friend of mine

You don't keep my best interest in mind

And because you're the only enemy Jesus doesn't want me
to love

Then I hate you!

With a passion!

Just like you Hate me,

But in the end you Lose

Boo Hoo

Boos for you because I'm cheerin' for Christ

But watch for that roaring lion out there ready and waiting
to take your life, shift you as wheat

Foreword

But if you're prepared and equipped then you can't be beat

Throw him unda' your feet and watch him squirm because he knows he's fresh meat

Belial

Don't be in denial

I thought you knew since Matthew that you've been destined to fail

Knowing Jesus Christ said, 'The gates of Hell will not prevail!'

Now go to Hell!

While I talk to the people of God

'Cuz see y'all

There's no time for indecision

Like Habakkuk we gon' write the vision

Ahh like Raven I just had a vision

I saw myself spelling the letters **B O L D E R**

Right in his face I said, 'Satan you're **BOLD**, but I'm **Bolder**

And as apart of his mission I saw him seeking to stop the spread of God's Word

Foreword

But Satan, there's JUST something about His Word 'cuz it
ain't leavin'

You think you can silence the Gospel

Well you just kuh keep on dreamin'

'Cuz we just figured out Blue's Clues

Man we don't need no Blue's Clues

To figure out what the wicked one is tryin' to do

'Cuz we're not ignorant to his devices

Mmmm I smell him and he's cookin' up something evil
throwin' in some unhealthy spices

But we're not gonna partake of his wine and daily bread
because we're demon intolerant

Yeah, that's what I'm hollerant

Gotta call out his bad, 'cuz he anit NO GOOD

Sinning from beginning God's throwin' in the wood

Stirrin' it up in that Lake of Fire

You tear my God down

But I Lift Him Higher and Higher

Foreword

And you may have power, but I ain't givin' you no
authority

God my King is the only one over me

Help you out?

Man, I'm lockin' you up

Make the devil cry and say, 'I get one phone call right?'

Wrong

Hasta la Vista baby

Chug the deuce and say so long

And we gotta treat him like that

'Cuz it's a fact that's he's steppin' up his persecution
because he knows short is his time

Ways to hinder your praise is runnin' through his mind

And we can't waste no more time, because the time is
already at hand

Don't wanna see my brothers and sisters drown in hell like
sinking sand

So let's take a stand

Here, grab my hand

Foreword

And If you have an ear, listen, aW is teaching, so that you
may be taught

You may not see it with your natural eyes, but A great
spiritual battle is being fought

So warning

For those of you who isolate yourself from other believers

Warning

For those you who are vulnerable in your faith

WARNING

For those of you who are spiritually weak

Search **BOLDLY** after God, so you won't be counted
amongst mediocre sheep

'Cuz all the devil wants to do is uproot your good and sow
some evil

I ain't jivin' y'all

Let's get WILD!

Like Evel Knievel

And sign up for our General Lord's recruit

Make the devil mad, hear him say man shoot!

Foreword

So jealous cuz we ain't apart of his crew

And even though everything may appear to be out of control

God is still in control, so everybody let's rock and rollllll!!

But know that, we can't unlock this **Boldness** by our lonesome

We need his Holy Spirit you better know son

'Cuz it's not by our power, and its not by our might, but on these battle grounds to be **BOLD**

It's by my Spirit saith the Lord.

Table of Contents

Introduction

Fasting is a very important aspect in our walk with God as believers. Fasting has been found to be beneficial in many different ways. I believe that this is why people of all backgrounds practice and believe in its power. Fasting has been used to gain insight, control weight, physical cleansing, and more. In Biblical times, fasting was during periods of time when individuals abstained from food for spiritual purposes. Have you ever, felt led by God to go on a fast? I felt encouraged to fast by the Lord and I recorded each day of my fast and I compiled them into this book. I now believe that everybody not just my friends need to hear this tell-all fast of a believer who is not perfect, but is striving for perfection in Jesus. I will call it the "Fasting Chronicles": What happened to me during my 40 days of fasting".

INTRODUCTION

In this book, I document my personal 40-day fast from beginning to end. You will get an uncensored look into my thought life and struggles during the 40 days of fasting. I will take you on a spiritual journey of a believer's true struggles and successes during this period of fasting. I often talk about the "elephant" in the room that everybody sees but refuses to acknowledge, because of the fear. This book will help believers that struggle with fasting to answer many of the honest questions that arise during this process. Take for example, how do I handle the evil thoughts that come during my time of fasting? How do I resist temptation of the mind and exercise spiritual discipline? How do I develop a Godly character? Who am I really? All of these questions and many more are documented in this book. Each event is true and my true thoughts and feelings at the time of writing this book.

INTRODUCTION

The origin of this work is quite unique. The work started from a desire that God had given me for our local church body. I am not the Pastor of the church, however I am a minister. I am a 'homemade' minister in that all of my training has come from God; I have never attended a seminary or theology school of any kind. I did attend college and I have three degrees: Bachelors of Science in Pure Mathematics, Master of Science in Applied Mathematics, Master of Sciences in Mathematics Education and at the time of this writing I have all but completed my dissertation for my PhD program in Mathematics Education. From my educational background comes my online nickname "Gospel Professor". As you can see I am not a stranger to education and I like to think of myself as a very logical thinker. I have learned through the years that with all my logical education, **God is only logical through the lens of the Holy Ghost.**

INTRODUCTION

As I began to prepare for my fast I was wondering within myself how could I ever commit to such a task, 40 days of no food? I had not been more than a day or two, at most, without anything to eat. This was not going to be easy and had to be God- inspired for me to attempt and complete. (I mean I loved food and it was obvious if you took a look at me standing 6'2" weighing 286.) Being committed spiritually was one thing; I questioned myself how could I go through with it physically. I admit as Christians we make bold claims and exercise faith, but I needed smart faith on this. Besides, if it was not done correctly or with God's anointing I could get seriously ill or even die. Then the Holy Spirit revealed to me how I should proceed ... write it all down.

In preparing for this fast I had decided that I wanted to document each day of my fast so that when it was over I could read back over it for inspiration to help me through tough times. So I began the fast, and started a private

online blog about what happened to me each day, how I

was feeling each day, and what my focus was each day.

After my first two entries, I knew I should share it with

others. I thought to myself why would anyone read it? But

I knew it had to be done.

While in school (high school, college, and graduate school)

I was quite popular because of athletics and student

government. The opportunity to serve others in these

capacities allowed me to make acquaintances with

thousands of people. I love meeting people; it could be a

hobby for me. Therefore, when I joined the social network

website Facebook.com, many of my high school and

college associates befriended me on the site. I had over

1,000 friends and about 98% of them I know on a first

name basis. I shared the blog with this community by

posting a link to it everyday. Before I knew it, I was

receiving comments and prayer requests from people on the website. I was amazed that people were actually reading this; and then God spoke to me. God said that there was a need for believers from every walk of life to hear from Him in this way, but many were not sure of what a fast was, how to go about it, and what the benefits were.

What an awesome position I was in ... the world's largest pulpit, the Internet. Many people wrote on my blog about how they have been inspired and how God was also pushing them to fast. The blog spoke to their lives. This book is a direct result of the daily fasting blogs. The blogs chronicle my 40-day fast ups and downs.

 The blogs helped me more than I realized; I often reviewed what I wrote for inspiration to myself. I posted pictures of myself on the website at three different stages of the fast: **day 1, day 21, and day 42**. I wanted everybody to see the glory of God upon my face through the physical manifestation of my body. Through the blogs, and encouragement from my Facebook family, I was inspired to finish the fast. I pushed to finish even more because I did not want to destroy their faith.

Like anything else the blog had and still has its critics. I have been openly rebuked from others saying that this was not a true fast and it was only to uplift myself. I was told things like: "A fast is supposed to be done only in secret." "You should not let others know what you are doing because it uplifts you."

I must admit, these comments were painful when they were first said, especially coming from people I trusted. However, from the fast I've learned that visionaries are not always liked nor understood. When you know what God has commissioned you to do, you learn to shake this type of stuff off and do what you are told to do.

I sincerely hope that you are impacted while reading this chronicle; that you are changed forever into what He desires for you to be, in JESUS name.

Sincerely,

Gospel Professor

Section 1

"Braxton-Hicks Contractions"

FEAR: **F**alse **E**vidence **A**ppearing **R**eal

DAY

1 of 40

Braxton-Hicks Contractions:

FEAR: False Evidence Appearing Real

Day 1 (9/29/09)

If it seems impossible to you, you're where God needs you

to be at the end of your strength, relying on Him.

Remember He's the God of all possibilities.

-Pastor Biggurs

To my readers I will give details and be as honest as possible about my spiritual journey. I am doing this fast for several reasons, which I will explain later in this entry. It is my goal to take you along and blog everyday of my fast. I feel that our society lacks honesty and people being transparent about life and spiritual issues. If someone has to stand out and make the first step, why not me?

Well I am no stranger to fasting; I have done it many times in many different ways for many different reasons. While in college, I fasted at least once a week for about a year but like most things somehow I got sidetracked. I believe by

FEAR: False Evidence Appearing Real

blogging and talking about this everyday it will encourage me to stick to it. You all are helping me as much as I hope that I am helping you.

The reasons for this fast are simple and, yet can be life changing to me. I have listed them below in order of importance to me:

1. Increased spiritual anointing and effectiveness in ministry. I want to prepare myself for new doors that God is about to open in my life. I want to put my body under subjection to the Spirit and make it a living sacrifice to God.

2. My marriage. We all have strongholds in our relationships and I am believing God to break these strong holds in our individual lives as well as our marriage. The strong holds of fear, anger, bitterness, resentment, strife, envy, abuse, etc. I can't name them all but He knows what they are. I am also fasting for the next generation that my

marriage will give birth to. I am believing God for children to be conceived soon and those children not to deal with the generational curses and strongholds that their parents (my wife and I) have dealt with.

3. Church family. My church family is great; however like any church family we all have our shortcomings. Our church is a unique place in that we have a diverse congregation, which can mean diverse problems. To be more specific -- problems that White people deal with on the surface seem different than the problems that the Black people deal with and the problems of Hispanic people are different from both of them. This puts the leadership of the church into some pretty emotional situations. So, I'm fasting for complete emotional healing of the leadership. This includes past hurts, mistrust, mistreatment, and bad members. I am also fasting for the emotional and spiritual healing of church members that have fought many battles

both spiritually and physically of racism and self-ism in church. I fast for one corporate body; a body that doesn't see color, and that will be willing to trust a brother or sister as if they were their own flesh and blood. I pray that they do not play favorites but seek God in all decisions and always do what is right for the whole and not the majority or minority.

I weighed and measured myself this morning --6'2" 283.6 lbs. I know throughout this fast I will lose weight, but I'll make sure I stay healthy. This is not designed to kill my body but to help feed my Spirit man. This week my reading is *Fasting* by Jentezen Franklin. (I read a lot so I will keep you posted as my readings change.) My goal is to let you into my mental world. I believe the best way to do this is to be honest and real about all situations. I am far from perfect, however I believe I have a tremendous call on my

life and I don't mind sharing my climb to spiritual success
with you.

My fast will consist of the following:

1. I will drink water as much as I want.

2. I will drink fruit juices as much as I want.

3. I will drink "Boost" or "Ensure" or 5Hour Energy to
keep my energy levels up, my goal is not to destroy my
health or body.

4. I will use breath mints such as Altoids or Tic-Tacs. I
work in an environment where I can't be blowing people
out with my breath and I have learned from previous fasts
that my breath stinks when I fast.

5. I will pray daily, for as long or as little as I feel.

5. I will not have food of any sort until 11/8/09.

6. I will not abstain from sexual activity with my spouse (I am on the fast not her).

7. During this time of fasting I will continue to work everyday. I am working on a couple of major projects also. I have to take my oral exam for my PhD on 10/6/09, keep me in prayer on that, it's big. I am also writing my dissertation proposal during this period also.

This fast will be different than the fasts I've done in the past, in that I will not have any food this time. The start date is 9/29/09. When I got up this morning my song of the day is CeCe Winans' *Everlasting Love.*

I'm ready with large quantities of water, juice and Boost. The one thing that is getting me is that I woke up this morning sneezing uncontrollably; which may indicate that I may be on the verge of being sick. So I guess that's stone number one the enemy is throwing at me -- sick on top of fasting! Whatever devil, I am pumped, let's do this. I am also on a *Facebook* fast, so I hope they all read my last status update and come to the blog.

Until tomorrow, if it's the Lord's will,

Gospel Professor

Day 2

At times we have to make a choice between pleasing God or pleasing people. The choice is simple: Please God, because people are never really satisfied.

Today is the second day of my fast. As I promised I will share with you things that happen to me during this fast spiritual, mental and physical.

As I told you yesterday I was going through those sneezing spells, it has now contributed to my headache. I sneezed more than 50 times yesterday -- hard. So hard I could feel muscle pains all over my body. Most would say this is a side-effect from the fast. At this point of course my mind tells me to quit fasting, get well, and try again later. However, my spirit says push and that's what I am going to do. My wife gave me some Clarinex and that has pretty much helped with the sneezing, but the headaches are still with me. I wanted to take something else for the headaches – like pills -- but my wife suggested that I do not take pills on an empty stomach but what she doesn't know is that I have been taking pills on an empty stomach for years, and it has never really bothered me. As of right now, I think I am having a sinus issue.

Before going to bed last night I read more of the fasting book and two more chapters this morning. This book has been very motivating to my faith and it pushed me to see what God will do when I do my part. I spent a lot of time on YouTube last night watching TD Jakes and the inspiring words he had to say. I enjoyed it until my Internet shut down ...

When I got up this morning I was convinced that I have gotten this cold from the ceiling fan that my wife insists has to run all night or she will sweat to death, while I feel like *Chilly Willie* wrapped up in every cover I can find.

Braxton-Hicks Contractions:

FEAR: **F**alse **E**vidence **A**ppearing **R**eal

When I got up this morning after a couple of midnight trips to the restroom from drinking too much water. I felt pretty good and my hunger was under control. I got on the scale and noticed I had lost about 3 lbs. The real difference I have seen so far was in prayer this morning. When I prayed I felt a flow that I have not experienced in a long time. It felt wonderful; I could feel God's love around me. I felt as if He was holding me in His arms and loving me. It was an intimate time with God. I am looking forward to what else the day will bring.

We have church tonight and I did not go to work today because my co-workers insisted that I stay home because of the constant sneezing yesterday, it was pretty bad. If I can just shake this headache then I will be fine.

Until tomorrow, if it is the Lord's will,

Gospel Professor

Day 3

God is absolutely just. He loves, and He forgives, but He doesn't compromise His righteousness. Live a life of no compromise; right is right and wrong is wrong.

Welcome back to my ongoing journal about my 40-day fast, today makes day three. I did not make it to work yesterday because of my head cold, however I am pleased to announce that it's pretty much gone. Yes!! It almost had me but I got away. There is always a way of escape I just had to PUSH (**P**ray **U**ntil **S**omething **H**appens) through it.

I went to church yesterday afternoon and I quickly learned about the power of the Internet. Many of you told me that you read about my fast and were encouraged. You also spoke of how God has challenged you to fast. I have been using the share button from my blog site to post this blog to my Facebook and Twitter accounts. So if it seems like I am logging in, that is what is happening. So don't think I am slipping -- LOL. But, I was challenged with temptation yesterday, and I made it through. Of course I will spill the details ...

... After church last night, my wife dragged me to Wal-Mart because she had to bake something for a friend. When I walked into the place all I could smell was the freshly baked bread from Subway. My wife went on and on about how good everything smelled and all the treats that Wal-Mart had all over the place. (If I have not told you, my wife doesn't really know that I am going on this fast for 40 days. All she knows is that I am fasting which I do a lot anyway but never for this long. I guess she will figure it out soon.) So we were shopping for food and my stomach is going crazy. It seemed like every treat was asking to be eaten right off the shelf. However, God did provide a way of escape. All of a sudden I had to go to the bathroom, and that was my chance to get away from temptation. Once I left the bathroom, I went to the magazine rack to read hunting magazines. I grabbed the latest issue, went back to my wife, and she continued to shop and get items while I had my nose buried in that hunting magazine. So I learned **not to take the little victories for granted because they lead to bigger ones.**

I have also noticed some changes in how I interact with my wife. It seems like she has been on edge a bit; however, I am discovering through this fast that, I may have been ignoring something deeper going on there. In other words I am becoming more sensitive to her. Sometimes, I do have to reevaluate myself to see if it was something I had done or said that made her react a certain way. I just have to remember that we wrestle not against flesh and blood but principalities. I do believe that maybe God could be dealing

FEAR: **F**alse **E**vidence **A**ppearing **R**eal

with her and I have to be sensitive to it. We all deal with things but we don't express them the same way.

God challenged me in giving today. But first, I must say that I have had people tell me in so many words that this blog has blessed their lives. My motivation for doing this is to let others know what real believers go through; that we are not holier, but we are just people that are led by the spirit. OK I am starting to preach, so back to God's challenge to me.

Out of the blue yesterday a guy that I know stopped by my house and rang my doorbell. I went to answer the door and I recognized he was an alumnus of the college I went to for undergrad. We talked about him coming by to do something to my lawn and discussed the price. Last night, God spoke clearly to me to double what I was going to pay him. At first I was thinking that I really needed this money, but then being humble and obedient because of the fast, I knew that he might need it more than me. What was funny was that the price he gave me planted a seed in my life. His seed grew in a couple of hours because God told me to give him double what he asked!

While I was reading a couple of chapters in my fasting book, I read about digging up seeds and how when we are not patient we dig up seeds before they get a chance to come up. I was so moved by it I felt the spirit tug on my heart and say that it needed to be heard by the gentleman that was working on my yard. So I photocopied that page in the book and enclosed the money in it, folded it tight and told him as I left to read it after he finished my yard. I also informed him that his money was inside of the paper. This is how God works. This man just called me at 11:28 am while I was writing about the challenge to you. I could tell in his voice that it was God moving on him. I will share what he said…

Braxton-Hicks Contractions:

FEAR: False Evidence Appearing Real

He said while he was plugging my yard for grass next year that God was speaking to him about his blessing being in the seeds he had sown and so on. To make a long story short he packed up his stuff after he finished and began to read the paper I had given him. It was complete confirmation to what God was telling him while he was working on my yard. WOW! Y'all this fast is really blowing my mind and its only day three. What else is God going to do? I love being a vessel but it's not easy. It takes a lot of self-sacrifice; however, it's so totally worth it.

I am sorry this is so long but I am so full today. I've got to tell you this last part. I begin praying this morning before I left. I felt so high in prayer I didn't want to stop. Many different people I know were coming to my mind and I was trying to bless them as quickly as I could. Believe it or not all of the people that came to mind were married couples.

They were couples from my past and present. I don't know what that means but I am sure God has a plan for them.

My energy levels are good. The Boost works wonders because of all the vitamins that are in it. I still fight hunger a little, and I don't waste time in the bathroom, LOL. My weight today is 278.2. I am losing about 3 lbs a day. I pray that the Lord keeps working on me. I hope someone was blessed through my transparency in my quest to be more like Him.

Until tomorrow, if it's the Lord's will,

Gospel Professor

Day 4

Whenever you set your heart to love, you open yourself up to hurt. Does this mean we shouldn't love? NO! That's how Christ loves us, and there's no greater LOVE!

I went home that afternoon and began to prepare for the party that my wife was baking for. When I got home all I could smell were sweets and baked goods, however they did not really bother me. The dinner party was pretty cool but the most important thing I got out of it was from the host of the party. The host of the party is an associate of mine that I am becoming quite fond of. He began to tell me how much he received when I preached a couple of weeks ago. The message was titled "Cash for Clunkers", and in it I talked about Hosea and Gomer's relationship and how it parallels our relationship with God *(Hosea 1)*. From there I made the connection to our natural world of how **no matter how bad we are if we are still living we have a chance to**

come back to God and thank him for the ultimate price He paid with his life. Thus … *Cash for Clunkers.*

He told me how that message made sense to him and how God was able to speak to him through me. From this experience, he said that he followed me to a conference I spoke at a couple of weeks later. I told him that I was shocked to see him at the conference because I did not think he made road trips. Again he informed me how he got the message from my presentation style, which he said was so different from the others he has always heard.

He said he felt like I was able to connect strongly with the younger audience, yet still have the older audience captivated by what I was saying. He said that everything I talked about was heartfelt. I confirmed that it was, because I preach and teach out of my experiences, joys, hurts and how I overcame them all. That is one of the main reasons for this fast is so that I can express to someone else with heart-felt conviction how important it is to practice fasting. I am often reminded by the old saying: *I can show you better that I can tell you.*

Talking to him was very encouraging. It was just what the doctor ordered. I have always struggled with my identity since I knew without a doubt that I was different. I often worried about my presentation style because it is not traditional. I can't sing, nor do I sound like Dan Rather when I speak. Most of the popular speakers can at least sing or have a great speaking voice. Then God had me to realize during a previous fast that I needed to use what he gave me. I knew I could talk circles around most anybody; I am a thinker, and a decent researcher. I thought, with these talents and my personality, how would this work? I can truly tell you that I still don't understand it, but with God's Anointing it works.

FEAR: False Evidence Appearing Real

The spiritual side of me is doing quite well. Due to work, I did not get to pray this morning like I would normally like to because I had to take my "program kids" on a field trip today (I am blogging to you while on the trip). However God did speak in two ways to me today. First, I am still reading the fasting book by Franklin that I mentioned earlier, and in it he spoke about how as you fast things begin to come out of you. Then he gave this story about a woman that somehow inherited an old home that needed to be cleaned and on the property was also an old well.

Her father used that well to throw away things that he did not want and it basically became a landfill. In order to clean the well out she hired some well cleaners. The well cleaners began their work and informed her when they were done. When she saw the pile of stuff she said to them that they were not finished and to keep going. This went on for a while … they would say that they were done and she would tell them that they were not. The well cleaners asked again if they were done one last time and the lady indicated that they were. Then the well cleaners asked, "How did you know when we were finished?" She said, "I knew when you pulled out that teapot, because it was the first thing that was thrown into that well when I was a little girl."

So she figured that the last thing out would have been be the first thing that was put in. Keeping that in mind, while I was in the shower this morning preparing for my field trip I reflected back to my first sexual encounter with a young lady that I met while in high school. This was one of the first things that started me down a path that was not becoming of me. Now the more I think about it that could have been the seed that was planted in me many years ago and God just uprooted it that quickly. Wow, what an awesome God!

Braxton-Hicks Contractions:

FEAR: False Evidence Appearing Real

The second thing that happened to me today was directly related to the previous occurrence. Since the first thing that you put in should be the last thing out, I have found out first hand that this is also physically. This morning right after I got ready to leave for work I got an upset stomach. I was wondering how could this happen when I have not eaten anything. So I used the bathroom and what I saw blew me away. I have never seen my stool so black in all my life. By fasting my body was eliminating all toxins and stuff that has been left in my body for years. It was crazy. I instantly felt better, so as you can see it works both physically and spiritually.

Last point and I'm done for today. I was riding on the bus for our field trip and I was thinking about the things I had mentioned earlier. Then I remembered when in the Garden, Adam and Eve committed the first sin by being disobedient and eating of the forbidden tree. Notice what I said: they were eating. If it were not for Adam and Eve eating, then we all would live forever, with God right? So take this nugget that I have today, "When you are not eating your body is healing itself". From my own experience thus far, I can attest to this fact. I have had joint pain in my shoulder for years from a football injury and it bothers me on the regular basis and I have a skin condition. Since the fast I have not had any pain or any issues with my skin. I feel great and full of energy. So could it be that we are literally eating ourselves to death? Is that why Jesus refers to fasting and praying so often? Could it be that the fountain of youth is within us and we are constantly clogging it up? Great questions, but what are the answers?

Braxton-Hicks Contractions:

FEAR: **F**alse **E**vidence **A**ppearing **R**eal

I got on the scale before I left this morning and I am now 276.2, I think that's down 2 lbs since yesterday. I just wanted to keep you up on that also.

Until tomorrow, if it's the Lord's will,

Gospel Professor

Day 5

Today is day 5 of my 40-day fast; I am doing well. In my body I can see visible changes; I can now see my rib cage slightly. I have not seen them since high school -- LOL. I am starting to understand different things about life and me during this fast so far.

I now truly understand that if I make up my mind to do something, I can really do it. There was a case of this in the Bible with the Tower of Babel. The people were determined to create a tower that reached the heavens and they would have succeeded if God did not confuse the languages. Interesting huh? (*You should read that story in Genesis 11:1-9).*

I did have to fight within myself not to eat something last night. I am to the point that I am not hungry but my mind keeps telling me that I need to eat. I have started day dreaming of eating and in some cases I thought that I was actually eating like a man having a wet dream. It was that real to me. So I clearly understand that the mind can and will play tricks on you. However, my spirit is greater than that and I just have to remain focused on the task at hand.

Since the fast I have not really slept through a night yet. It has not been the bathroom breaks, but I have just woken up a couple of times. I have felt the urge to pray for a couple of people today so I did do that. I had to get up early again this morning because I had a meeting with my "program kids" again today. I was wondering what encounter would I have today because I have pretty much had one everyday, as you have read. On my way to work I noticed a woman at the bus stop with her back turned to me. As soon as I passed the bus stop I immediately knew who it was without seeing her face. I knew I should go back and pick her up, but I kept telling myself that I was already late for work.

Braxton-Hicks Contractions:

FEAR: **F**alse **E**vidence **A**ppearing **R**eal

Then I got convicted because I knew that I controlled how things in my program would run and if I were not there they would not start without me. So I pulled over and turned around and went back to the bus stop.

Yep it was exactly who I thought it was, I asked her where she was heading and if she needed a ride. She got in and we rode to the store. She needed to go to on the other side of town. (I must note that I have ministered to this lady many times, because she is a member of our church. I say that to say that I was already familiar with her situation, it was not divine intervention or anything even though I believe it can and has happened to me.)

She began to talk about things that were going on in her life and also about friends of hers. (I don't know yet what the purpose of me picking her up was. Maybe she needed to see me or maybe I was confirmation, better yet was God testing my patience and was I really willing to put His needs first instead of my own)? I wonder how many times does God put us in this position? A chance for us to be blessed or a chance to be a blessing to someone else? I remembered when I was a teenager I walked most places I needed to go. So I made a pact with myself that if I ever saw anybody that I knew walking and they needed a ride, then I would provide it. I understand how it is to be in those shoes and I am grateful that I am no longer in that situation.

The last thing I wanted to talk about was while my "program kids" were in class today, I went to look at my favorite TV station, YouTube, man you can find just about anything on it. I don't quite remember how I picked this particular video but it was Oprah talking to Larry King about the book "The Secret". I remember when this book first came out there was a lot of talk about it. As I watched about three other videos about it, the Lord began to speak to me about it. The book revolves around the idea of the law of attraction and how we are energy and we attract things to ourselves -- thus our future is based on what we attract. Then almost instantly it came to me: Why is this being disguised as the "secret"? This stuff is in the Bible and there is nothing secret about it. The Bible gives all of these secrets. It never amazes me how people will pay tons of money to quickly fix all their problems when the Bible provides the solution to them all.

My physical health seems to be well; I weighed in this morning at 274.2. I am still losing weight, about two pounds a day.

Until tomorrow, if it's the Lord's will,

Gospel Professor

Day 6

Well what can I say, another amazing day. I am starting to wonder if everyday of my life has always been like this and I am just starting to notice since the beginning of my fast. It seems like everyday since I started fasting, the most amazing things have been happening to me. What I am thinking is maybe these things have been happening all of the time but I was never sensitive to them until I started this fast. I find that very interesting.

When I weighed myself today I was 272.2 so I am down 2 lbs. from yesterday. I was caught off guard this morning with a bowel movement; I guess my body is still cleansing itself, as it renews itself. Today is Sunday, which means I attend church today and of course I have to let you know what happens to me. I will also let you into my thinking and some of the things that God allowed to be on my mind today and late last night.

Braxton-Hicks Contractions:

FEAR: False Evidence Appearing Real

I finished the fasting book by Franklin last night; it was a great book and it has helped me tremendously in my fasting efforts and I would recommend it to anyone reading this blog/book if you are going on a fast. I have noticed that fasting is forcing me to go to bed earlier, when I usually stay up late. I figured that my body needs the extra rest since it is repairing itself physically, mentally and spiritually.

When I got to church today it was pretty normal, with the exception of our guest speaker, who was a prophet. I thought to myself, 'What timing, I am on a fast and the prophet is in town.' I know many people don't believe in prophets and I would admit that I, at times, have had my doubts, not in prophets but in those who claim to be them. I validate them by measuring them up against what the Word of God says they should be. If they measure up according to the Bible fine, if they don't I am weary of them and you should be too. However, this prophet gave a word of hope and inspiration of what God has done and what He is still able to do.

Then, he began to prophesy over others. In my opinion, prophesy should only confirm what God already told me. (That's my opinion, so you can take that for what it's worth to you.) Prophecy can also be very dangerous if the person prophesying is not a true prophet. Why? If a person claiming to be a prophet came in and told you that you were going to get a million dollars at the end of the month and if that month comes and goes by without you getting that million dollars a few things might happen: Your faith in that person is destroyed, it can harm your faith in God because you believed this person to be from God, and it can cause a person to make some decisions that they would not have normally made based on the words of the "false prophet".

FEAR: **F**alse **E**vidence **A**ppearing **R**eal

This brings me to what actually happened to me today. When the offering time during the service came the prophet asked eight people to give offerings of $209; from there he asked others to give $109. There came a point while he was walking around handing out envelopes to people to give $109 that he came to me and said that I was to give $109. I told him that I did not have it and refused an envelope. He then asked me if I had faith and I told him yes but I know that I did not have the money. So he told me to take the envelope and if I did not have it by service tomorrow then he would give it to me.

Needless to say this was a very awkward situation for me. Yes I do give; I give everything that I have. I am sold out, literally. I have been a tither and offering-giver all of my life, ever since I got my first job. I currently give 12% tithes and 6% offering from my gross and yes God has always provided for me. God challenged me a couple of years ago to give this way. It may not be for everybody, but it works for me. Needless to say, I felt awkward and somewhat embarrassed because I didn't have the money, and I didn't feel that God told me to give it. However, I did believe that God knows my heart and He would provide for me to be able to give the $109 if it's His will.

I don't find it funny that I have started reading a new book called "God's Secret to Greatness: David Cape, and Tommy Tenney talk about serving others and using the power of service to be great. I have only read the first chapter but I look forward to reading the rest. **God is slowly preparing me for something, just pray that I hang in there and don't dig up the seed.**

Until tomorrow, if it's the Lord's will,

Gospel Professor

Day 7

Today is day 7 of my 40-day fast. I feel well and everything seems to be all right. I weighed this morning and I weigh 270.2 that's another 2 lbs loss. It seem like my body has been pretty consistent in my weight loss. I report and monitor this as a way to calculate my health and to make sure there were no major changes to quickly. By most people's standard; two pounds a day is major but I am looking for something like eight or more, then I would have cause for concern.

I must confess that I have logged onto Facebook a couple of times to check on this blog and I had a couple of urgent inbox messages, like two deaths this week in my former church. Therefore, I repent and confess for logging onto Facebook. The main reason I fasted from Facebook was because it was a distraction for me, nothing more and nothing less. I get more done when I am not spending hours on it.

I took off work today so that I can review for my oral exam tomorrow at NC State. This is the last exam before I officially start to write my dissertation. Please pray that it goes well for me. It has been a long time coming with that. I have not gotten to study as much as I wanted because I have had so many things to do.

I also needed to wash clothes, so I'm beginning to clean out my closet and rid it of things that were wore out or no longer needed. It was funny as I was doing this I thought about the parallels of it. I was physically cleaning my closet out and God was spiritually cleaning me out. I also welcomed the benefits of the fast. I saw several items that I had purchased brand new and other old items that I had put away; I can comfortably wear all my clothes in my closet now. This will most likely be short lived because I have estimated that I will probably shed about 70+ lbs according to the pace my body has set so far.

I started this morning thinking about what had occurred yesterday with the prophet. I was wondering if I had failed a test. What I mean is: was God trying to give me an opportunity to fill my empty vessel and I refused by not taking the envelope initially? After I thought about it last night, I remembered some of the things that I was reading and I remembered reading that fasting is one strand of a three-strand cord. The other strands are prayer and giving. I have been praying and fasting but I had not done any giving except to the guy who worked on my lawn. When I go back to church tonight I will give the $109. It's literally my last.

I usually have the rainy day fund but because of different things I have used some of it. I was planning on maybe using it to celebrate my marriage anniversary this weekend

Braxton-Hicks Contractions:

FEAR: False Evidence Appearing Real

(7 yrs); however, I am trusting the Lord. It will be all right, the upside is all of my bills for the month are paid and I am not eating anyway, so I will be good. I don't want to miss out on something for my family or church family because I was too tight to give. When you give your last He knows, but I struggle with that too. God knows my heart and why I'm going to give it; I will let Him do the rest.

On another note I got the meaning of what happened to me on Saturday. Remember when I was telling you about the lady that I picked up and took to the store before work? Well, I was reading a book by Dave Cape and Tommy Tenny and the answer was within the pages. Dave gave a similar story of how he was washing this lady's feet in a similar situation to mine and spoke of how it was just a test from God to test his humility. As soon as I read that it hit me like a ton of bricks … that's what He was trying to do. I'm not going to lie to you, I am looking for something really great to happen before the end of the day. Not to say that the things that have already happened were not great but, it's Day 7, I have never fasted this long before, and I have a spirit of expectancy.

One last thing, I really appreciate the encouragement that I am receiving from my readers.

The comments are heartfelt and if God is inspiring you through me then go for it. We are living in a radical time so radical methods must be employed. **When my struggles with hunger come, I log on and read the comments that some of you have made and it keeps me committed, so keep commenting.**

Until tomorrow, if it's the Lord's will,

Gospel Professor

Day 8

Setbacks and delays are not denials; they are only moments of further preparation. Don't let the enemy tell you otherwise.

What can I say? I knew God had something special in store for last night and I know He does for the rest of my day today as well. As you can tell today is day 8. I never would have made it without God. I never pictured myself fasting so long. The road ahead is still long, but I have faith that I will make it through with God and the encouragement of the saints. Last night I saw a glimpse of another reason why I have been called to this fast. I will explain ...

God is an on time God all of the time, His timing is always perfect. I admit I was going in with a spirit of expectation last night as we went to church. Now since I have had a chance to examine my motivation it was selfish.

53

I was looking forward to what I thought God would do for me through the prophet, service, etc. However, I am learning daily that the true meaning of the fast is not about the enemy; it's about the inner me. When God does something for me He does it through me, not necessarily for me. I learned this last night on the job.

The service at church started pretty normally and a great word was given about the five porches at Bethesda -- the porches of: forgiveness, healing, miracles, spiritual breakthrough, and financial restoration. Little did I know that we would see all of these in one night. Well at least in my opinion we did. It is funny to me now but as I was reading Dave Cape and Tommy Tenny's book yesterday, I read a section where Tenny talked about a Spirit of giving breaking out in a place where he was when people were just emptying their pockets to give to one another. As I read that yesterday, I thought how awesome would that be if that happened in my church one night. Well, it did -- last night! While the prophet was preaching a lady in the congregation came up and threw five one hundred dollar bills at his feet. (I sit in the front row so I was able to clearly see them and count them lol.) I was amazed. Next thing I knew another person comes up and throws money at his feet, then another, then the prophet emptied out his pockets in front of everyone and at this point the spirit is all over the church. People come from everywhere emptying out their pocketbooks wallets, etc. It was great and also the beginning of financial restoration. I did not have much myself, all I had was the $109 dollars that I said I would bring before but I also got my wife to write a check for $209 that he asked for later, I will have to tap into some other sources that I was vowing not to touch but when the spirit is in the house like that you got to jump on it, besides I can't take it with me to heaven. What God allowed to happen next takes the cake...

FEAR: **F**alse **E**vidence **A**ppearing **R**eal

At this point we are at the altar seeking God for spiritual breakthrough, healing, forgiveness, etc. The Spirit of the Lord was high and in my mind I thought we were getting ready to leave. I think that is what everyone else thought too -- besides it was Monday night and that meant Brett Favre and the Vikings on prime time TV. God had a change of plans. Right before it seemed like we were about to be released to go home, our Pastor asked the prophet to pray with a young lady in our congregation. As he began to pray for her I assisted him, as I usually do but this time it was a little different. I clearly noticed a demonic force upon the young lady. All of the signs of something evil going on were present. I must tell you upfront that demons are nothing to play with if you are not: fasted up, prayed up, or if you are scared.

For me I was cool with the first two for sure, but I was a little scared because these are always a bit scary to me --

56

we are talking about someone else's life being taken over by a spirit that we cannot see. During my lifetime I have seen demons cast out of people several times and I have participated on the limited basis due to some of the things I told you before. However, I knew that God has been training me in this area for some time; therefore I studied the subject extensively and bought almost every book that was worthwhile on the subject and how to deal with a situation like this. In my opinion, the most famous books on this subject called *Pigs in the Parlor* by Frank and Ida Hammond.

This book has been around for at least 30 years or more. I remember as a child when I was about four or five years old, my father had this book in the house. I remember the cover of the book had pigs on it that were on top of the eye of another pig of some sort. I encountered this book at least three more times before I read it. I remember once in college I saw this same book being read by one of the barbers in the barbershop he was a young guy probably not even 30. He died not long after I saw him reading that book that day. So I was always kind of afraid to read this book. When I spoke with my father I asked him if he had the book and he spoke of it being long gone because he had loaned it out to someone. I had always purposed to get it and then one day when my parents came to visit my father said that he had something for me and it was that book. I said all of that to say that it's a powerful book. I also read books by Bishop George Bloomer on this subject as well. He is known for his gift in this area of ministry.

Back to the young lady … as we began to pray for her it seemed like we had little effect at first but then God brought back to my memory all I had learned from my readings. As I began to recall some of the techniques that were discussed in the books, things began to change. To make a long story short, we started to command the

demons to identify themselves and they did -- one by one.

At my last count there were ten that each gave their name.

After this we asked for the head demon to come forth and

he went by the name Alan. At this point most people would

have thought that this young lady went off the deep end. No

she was under the influence of demonic spirits. As time

went on we found out that they had been there for years.

Some of these spirits were accepted in many different

ways. In this particular case some could have come in

voluntary/involuntary through sexual contact. (Yes spirits

can transfer from sexual contact; that's another reason why

you should not fornicate even though I myself have been

guilty of it in the past.)

The demons that she picked up through sexual contact

could not leave until she forgave. They were holding her in

torment because she had not forgiven the people she had

been involved with and for what they had done to her. Next were demons of her childhood from painful childhood experiences. Then there were demons of music. I have learned that demons that enter in through music have to leave through music. As a result the ladies that were assisting the other gentleman and I began to sing holy songs; you could physically see the demon leaving the young lady. Most of the time the signs are rolling back of the eyes in the head and an open mouth; sometimes they stick their tongue out at you, and other times the eyes are wide open to the point where it seems like they may pop out of the person's head. It was truly an amazing night where we saw all of the five porches that the prophet had preached about in one service.

There is a lot more detail that I could go into but I will not. I was physically drained. Maybe that's why I need the weight loss so that I can be in better shape when these situations come. My weight today -- to my surprise -- is the same as yesterday. No loss at all -- 270 on the head.

It says in the Bible that, "this kind only leaves by fasting and prayer" *(Mark 9:29)*. If I was not fasting God could not have used us to help this young lady. I ask that you continue to pray for her that she stays protected.

So what does God have in store today? I pray that passing my oral exam today is in His will. I am about to travel to Raleigh, NC right now to take my final oral exam today so that I can begin my dissertation. Pray for me. I hope that God has moved upon you today.

Until tomorrow, if it's the Lord's will,

Gospel Professor

Day 9

Are you persuaded that God will do what He promised? If so, don't let what today looks like bring doubt, just be still and know God will do what He promised.

Well today is day 9 and I am still going forward. I am finding out how boring it can be when you are not eating. I have realized that eating takes up a lot of time. I have not been hungry much today, I did have a bout or two of hunger last night, but I survived. I weighed today and I am exactly 270 the same from yesterday. So this tells me that my body has definitely switched to burning fat reserves for energy. I can visibly tell my weight loss and when I came back to work today I was getting compliments on how young I looked all of a sudden -- Thanks God. Of course that helped boost my ego today -- like I need any help with that.

Braxton-Hicks Contractions:
FEAR: **F**alse **E**vidence **A**ppearing **R**eal

When I finished yesterday's blog post, I was headed to Raleigh to defend my oral exam that I have been raving about for the last week. Well, I tested and answered the questions to the best of my ability and the favor of God came out on top again. Did you really expect anything different? To be perfectly honest I had faith but I would be lying to you if I did not say the spirit of *Doubting Thomas (Read the story John 20:27)* did come upon me, but God took care of business -- I PASSED ... PRAISE THE LORD!

I cannot begin to tell you how happy I am about this. I have been working to get my PhD part time for about six plus years now. I still have to write the dissertation, which will take another year or so, and then I will most likely graduate December 2010. The part that most people don't get through is over so that's why I am so happy. God is so awesome!

I must also tell you that I was severely tempted last night to stop this fast. Even though God has done all of these truly awesome things in my life and other things through me, the human side of me wants to stop. It was telling me, "Hey God has hooked you up so why are you still fasting, and you got everything you wanted almost." I don't know about you but my flesh speaks to me like that sometimes. I had to get that off me. I am reminded about what Franklin said in his book that if you are spraying for bugs one time that you will kill the visible ones, but what about the ones you cannot see and the eggs that are not hatched. Now I've got to stay focused so I can kill the stuff that I cannot see the eggs of the ones that have not hatched … this is the tough part; not seeing sounds a lot like faith *(Hebrews 11:1).*

Lastly I have decided to mark this milestone in my life with something significant to me. If you look throughout the Bible when significant things happen or people went through tough times it was marked with something to help

them remember what happened. Like Jacob wrestling with

the angel he walked with a visible limp the rest of his life

(Genesis 32:25) and when the children of Israel crossed the

Jordan they made a monument *(Joshua 4:7)* and when

prodigal son came home his father gave him a ring (*Luke*

15:22).

I have decided to get a custom signet ring made of white

gold with a single diamond. The ring will have the *Finding*

Fish logo from my ministry and the eye of the fish will be a

diamond. One side of the ring will have a cross and on the

other side it will have the Star of David. Each of these

symbols has significant meaning to me. The inside of this

ring will bear an inscription that will read the *Fast that*

Birthed 9/29/2009 – 11/08/09. A signet ring is significant

because it was the seal of the king and only he had it. If you

had a document bearing the seal it meant that you were

with the king or you had an order directly from the king. At the end of this I want to be able to say that I have been with the true King and I have the seal to prove it.

When I was in the shower this morning God brought back to my memory that the number nine is the number of new beginnings, for me. I thought hard about that. I started the fast on 9/29/09 and the prophet said that God told him that the month of September this year was the month of "birthing". Without knowing that I started this fast, and this year has been my most productive year in ministry to date. This year my website www.daJesusProject.com came into existence as I had envisioned and I finished my PhD class work and I have started the birth of a new area of my life.

Braxton-Hicks Contractions:

FEAR: **F**alse **E**vidence **A**ppearing **R**eal

I am looking for more to happen before the year is out. However, I will stop and leave it up to God. Only He knows how to outdo Himself.

Until tomorrow, if it's the Lord's will,

Gospel Professor

Finding Fish Signet Ring

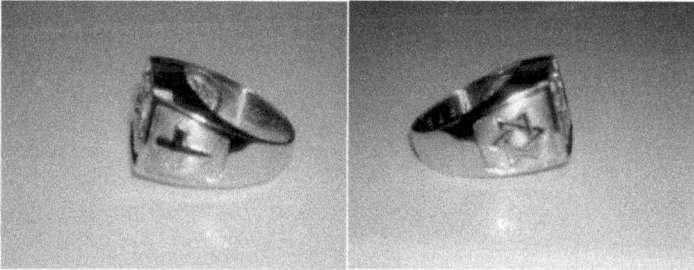

Day 10

God's mercy is new every morning. So if you are reading this text, SHOUT now, because you have New Mercy today.

Today marks day 10 of my 40-day fast. I have made it 1/4th of the way. I thank God for that. I weighed today, I came in at 268. That is down 2 lbs from yesterday. I also got another surprise today in that I had a bowel movement, since I have not eaten in ten days this was a surprise. I guess my body is still eliminating toxins and other harmful things in my body. I have two things that have been on my heart to address today: One is about what happened Monday night in the deliverance service in which we were helping the young lady and the second is about the attack on marriages across our region.

FEAR: False Evidence Appearing Real

It was quite a disappointment when I received the news that the young lady we were ministering to with the satanic strongholds on her life was admitted to the hospital. I was thinking to myself, "Lord why and what happened?" I was thinking about it later that night and while in another deliverance service working with another man that night.

After referring to, "*Pigs in the Parlor*" by Frank and Ida Mae Hammond, when I opened it God directed me straight to a chapter in the book called *Schizophrenia.* Not a lot is known about this "demonic disease", but we do know that it makes people believe they have multiple personalities. I am kicking myself now; I should have noticed that about that young lady immediately. It upsets me because I had the tools and did not apply them properly in this case. I hate missing opportunities; however, I will never forget that now. From this book, Ida Hammond received a revelation from God on how to deal with it.

FEAR: False Evidence Appearing Real

After reading what she wrote I now understand that it is a process to help a possessed person be fully free (I do believe in instant deliverance also). This person showed all of the symptoms. According to Hammond, Schizophrenia starts with rejection and usually happens at a very young age. The person is fighting this in the middle of all of these personalities. This is referred to in the book of James where they talk about a person of, "double mind is unstable in all their ways" *(James 1:8)*. What is happening is that the different personalities are taking control at different times. The reason it takes so long to get delivered is because the demons are all nested together. It took time for them to invite others in and to get to this point and to reverse it will take the same. The authors have been successful at helping individuals that had schizophrenia become whole again. Hearing that brings great promise that God can make her whole again. I will continue to pray and hope that if I come across a situation like this again that I will be better prepared.

Point two today, hurts me to my heart. I am seeing more and more couples that are having some serious marital issues. God, something's got to give! Here yesterday in Winston, NC we had a domestic violence disturbance that was taking place in a public restaurant and ended with the man dying. In Raleigh yesterday, about 6:30 a.m., a similar domestic violence situation occurred with a mother of two losing her life in front of her kids and the father attempting to take his own life. AHHHHH ...

I have to ask God what's up? What can we do? This is hard for us because many of us are fighting these very same battles, whether married 1 year or 20 years; we all are under attack! What is in the atmosphere that is causing these problems, were they always there and we are just starting to notice? Is the pain becoming so great that we would rather end it for both parties? Lord help us all. What must we do so that we can get along? What must we be willing to compromise to become one flesh, not just physically but emotionally and mentally? How do we sustain it? How do you get to the point where a human life is precious to us again? What happened to spouses wanting to please each other and as a result please You Lord? Lord, I have so many questions but no answers. I feel the frustration in the atmosphere; help us to kill the "eggs" that we don't see. That's now another reason for this fast -- killing the unseen *(Ephesians 6:11-12)*.

Like Daniel, I believe God sent the answer the first time, I asked but I have to help strengthen my faith through fasting and prayer.

Until tomorrow, if it's the Lord's will,

Gospel Professor

Section 2

Dilation of the Birth Canal

Stretching: Stopping To Repeatedly Embrace Thoughts Coming to Help Inspire Nobility & Greatness

Day 11

Because of the death of Christ on the cross our lives are not our own. We have been brought with a price: The CROSS.

I was glad when they said unto me let us go into the house of the Lord. Welcome to day 11 of the 40-day fast. I am still holding on. The last couple of days have been tough. I have really been hungry and it didn't help when I woke up to the smell of eggs and bacon in the house this morning. However, we each have our cross to carry and I am carrying mine. My weight today is down 1 lb today, 267. I feel fine and prayer was good this morning. I felt clear and free.

I went hunting yesterday to relax and sleep a little. It's nothing liking going to sleep in the woods. It's the most peaceful thing but dangerous since I am hanging from the side of a tree holding a weapon in my hand. I saw one deer

77

but it was running because it seems that some of the

neighbor's dogs took chase throughout the woods today for

exercise. Needless to say, I was not happy with that and

wanted to put a couple of them out of their misery, but then

I saw a mental image of the Michael Vick saga and decided

against it. Needless to say, that messed up my hunt and I

left early because deer will not come anywhere near where

a dog has been within a certain amount of time, and it was

getting dark.

While I was meditating today another old adage came to

mind; today it was, *Absolute Power = Absolute Corruption.*

As I was meditating on what that really means, I could not

help but think of the current situation that our world is in.

From the many dictators around the world to the dictators

that rule our country in our wonderful democracy (no I did

not contradict myself I mean that). Without the wisdom of

God it is harmful for one person or organization to hold all of the cards. As long as we are in the body we will have evil thoughts and may succumb to these things.

When I was younger I heavily study the history of Egyptians and Pharaohs. The things they discovered and how they got to rule always fascinated me. Many of the Pharaohs were boy rulers and did not truly rule until they were older.

The reason I brought them up was if you have noticed the headdress of many of the Pharaohs you would notice that it would have a snake (King Cobra) usually around it. This served as a reminder to the Pharaohs that every man has evil thoughts (the snake represented evil). To make things more interesting, in the Old Testament a snake wrapped on a stick represented healing for the children of Israel (*Numbers 21:9*).

It's clear to me that there is a very fine line between good and evil and we all have been on either side of it, or in the middle at times.

God sets things up so that we all need each other. I don't have it all nor do I know it all, but what I do know, I know well. When you put all of those things together in the body of Christ, for each believer, we form the Bride without spot or wrinkle that the Bible speaks about (*Ephesians 5:25-30*). If we are all the best at what we do, and all of that is put together to make the whole, who can stop it but the Father himself?

Until tomorrow, if it's the Lord's will,

Gospel Professor

Day 12

I was a little late writing today, I apologize, but I have had a very busy day. Today marked day 12 of the 40-day fast and I am out of town to celebrate my wedding anniversary at Myrtle Beach. SC. I can't think of a better setting to be writing to you from today. I do not have a weight report because I am not able to get on my home scale so I will update that with you when I get home.

This week has been a very challenging week for a number of reasons. The week started with a bang. We had a good church service on Monday night and I passed my PhD. exam on Tuesday. However, as the week went on my zeal of this fast started to decrease and my hunger for food increased. I am glad to say that I did not cheat but of course I thought about it several times. Heck, I am thinking about it right now, but when I think about that temporary satisfaction versus the long term things of God -- I force myself to continue. That's how you have to look at your walk with Christ. Do I give up my future for a short-term satisfaction? I can tell you it's not worth it. Think about all of the guilt that you would feel and how many other people would be let down. I know the fast is between Jesus and I but, I know He has and is still using my fast to inspire hope into others that they too should fast and pray for longer than a shorter period of time.

Being that I am celebrating my anniversary, of course I wanted to eat and enjoy this time with my wife and be full of energy, but I did not. I am thankful for my wife understanding and being humble during this period. It's been tough, both for her and myself, because when we go to Myrtle Beach we usually spend a lot of time in restaurants together. You would be surprised by what you can do when you really have a made up mind to do the right thing. Chicken broth was added to my fast today, I found it to be water with a chicken flavor, but it was like eating a steak to me. I never knew that the stuff tasted so good. It really helped to bring the energy level back up and stabilize my blood sugar level. I did also buy vitamins and some super green pills to help with my energy level and to make sure my body is getting everything that it needs. Remember I am not trying to kill my body, just my flesh.

My main thought today is about patience and frustration. I battle with these two concepts in all aspects of my life. You may have this battle also. They seem to be on opposing ends of the spectrum but somewhere in the middle hope exists. What is patience? It is defined as an ability or willingness to suppress restlessness or annoyance when confronted with delays. What about frustration? Frustration is a feeling of dissatisfaction, often accompanied by anxiety or depression, resulting from unfulfilled needs or unresolved problems.

I have been told many times that I am a very impatient person; that I should just wait. But my problem is not really waiting, it is waiting without an end somewhere in sight. Take for example if you tell me that you will pay me on Friday then I can wait until Friday and then I expect to be paid. But, what drives me nuts is when you tell me that I will pay you, but I don't know when but just trust that you will. How do you deal with that? This drives me to my second point, which is frustration. It brings feelings of anxiety and anxious wonderings when it is going to happen. Will it happen? Is the person who said that they would come through really deliver? That's why hope is in the middle of the spectrum on this because you have to have hope to stop frustration, but if hope does not exist then frustration sets in and when it is finished it usually leads to anger because of lack of control. Once you reach anger you have loss.

One should always hope because faith is the substance of things *hoped* for and the evidence of things not seen (*Hebrew 11:1*). What happens when you get tired of hoping for that person, thing or situation? Did it mean that you did not have faith? Of course not! But I have learned, it's the risk you have to take. So the real question is not whether you believe or not, but how much risk you are willing to take. Take for example, my risk to share my spiritual struggle with the world through this blog/book in the making. I actually find it almost therapeutic to be able to say exactly how I feel it.

Most people do this all of time but for a true believer like myself to be candid with you without fear of repercussions from others or public back lash, is quite a relieving experience. It's amazing that being a man of God, I could talk in front of thousands of people and give sound advice and then be blessed with the satisfaction to see them prosper from it. Yet sometimes I feel like a failure in my own home, not that I don't live what I preach. The point is that I have to live it first and make all of the mistakes so that I can give you the good advice from my experiences.

I am often reminded of something that a young lady told me in college about experience and it went like this: *Experience is a tough teacher. It gives the test first and the lesson later.* When I minister or give advice to someone it's usually not what I think. My advice comes from data that was collected in the field by me. So stand on the shoulders of "Giants in the Faith" and learn from the mistakes of others. It pushes you that much further forward, because the next generation depends on your success.

If God was water, then when things are hot He can steam up your situation. When things are cold He will be solid like a rock and when things are not freezing or steaming it can be enough to satisfy your thirst for Him.

Until tomorrow, if it's the Lord's will,

Gospel Professor

Day 13

Today was a different day. During my ride home today I had a lot of time to think. While I was riding and reflecting on my weekend thus far, God dropped in my Spirit some more things about my fast. This fast has four different parts, which represents a spiritual birth that is going on and it's a 40-day process. The first ten days of the fast is: Braxton-Hicks Contractions, then the Dilation of the birth canal, then Pushing and finally the Birth.

The **Braxton-Hicks Contractions** stage days 1-10 of the fast are the parts of the fast that deals with the things that I could see. If you recall the first ten days of the fast were all praise reports. Everyday I told you stories of different things God had done and how He was opening doors and moving on my behalf in certain situations. Like Braxton-Hicks Contractions, these things were good but they were not the real thing. It was good that God took care of all of these things, but I can't focus on these things because they are superficial. The fast itself is much deeper than this. Most of us would be satisfied with this stage but it's temporary -- it's only preparing you for the birthing process, which is so much more. Sometimes you get pain during this stage, but you overlook it because the excitement of the new things that God is allowing to happen is so refreshing.

The **Dilation stage** happens during days 11-20. During this period the birth canal is being prepared to birth what God has for you to do. Like in child bearing, this process can be painful. The stretching that God allows you to go through is incredible. Things that you did not believe you could go through you go through them. You feel like God is not near but life is ever present -- shooting its fiery darts at you.

The next stage is the **Pushing stage** days 21-30. In the pushing stage you are fighting to get out what God wants to give to the world. The things that have been stored up inside of you for the kingdom are starting to be recognized and you start to gain confidence in your abilities. This is a developmental stage of ministry. The way you P.U.S.H. is: (**Praying Until Something Happens**). God is already in position to help us bring life to our gifts, but we have to be humble to see His ways. Therefore we have to **PUSH.**

The final stage is the actual **Birth**, days 31-40. In this stage we actually give complete birth to our ministry or calling as a result of consecrations, praying and fasting. This is when God reveals to the world your light and what He wants you to do for Him. You are now prepared to be the Salt of the world. Your gifts will make room for you (*Proverbs 18:16*).

What happened to me today was truly unexpected. After my trip I dropped my wife off at home and was heading to my parents house to go to a funeral the next day. While driving, the Spirit spoke to me and it said for me to turn around and go home. I was not sure that it was the right

spirit (other spirits do speak to you sometimes but you have

to make sure that it's the right spirit). So I said, "God if it is

You, I need a sign." Keep in mind I was driving down the

highway. Then I said, "Lord if this is You then somebody I

have not talked to in years will call me on the phone." So

as I drove down the highway, about five minutes later my

phone rang. I did not recognize the number but I thought it

was my mother so I answered and to my amazement it was

my cousin that I had not heard from in over ten years.

Needless to say, that was enough for me. If I could have

whipped that car around in the middle of the interstate I

would have. Once I got a chance to turn around, God spoke

to me again and said to stop by an old friend's house that

was very close to where I was. I understand in hindsight

that this was the real purpose of my trip.

While at my old friend's house, we shared laughs about old

times and his father began to talk to me about different

things. As we began to talk God spoke through him to me about several things that were a confirmation to me.

The one thing that stood out the most was that I needed to be supremely confident in God and what He was doing with my life (*2 Corinthians 5:4-8*). He said that my fasting is positioning me for what God wants to bring me into. What God has for me is much larger than I would have ever set for myself. If I did it people would say it was by my power, but if He does it then they will have to acknowledge that it was God and His plan for me. I was reminded that the way I thought I was going to go was not the way I was going and that God has another way mapped out for me. God is honoring my fast and I have to remember that He will help me out of my hurt.

God is truly awesome, every time I think I am doing one thing; God surprises me with another, like what I just described.

I thought I was going to see my parents and God sent me

on a detour for a word He need planted in me. **I've got to**

hold out and be SUPREMELY CONFIDENT IN GOD.

Until tomorrow, if it's the Lord's will,

Gospel Professor

Day 14

Adversity is simply God's school of promotion. Count it all joy when you find yourself in trials and tests. Knowing this: once you pass, promotion is on the way.

What can I say I have made it to day 14. I got on the scale this morning and I weighed 266, that's down two more pounds since the last time I weighed in. God has been good to me. I feel that I have made it through some rough spots and I am strong, however I still have not made it half way yet. These days are the days of God stretching me, in faith, giving, and prayer. I took it easy today and spent some time with my wife at home. I went to church tonight as well to listen to the word that God had for me.

While in church God spoke to me -- it seems like the Lord speaks to me at the oddest times. God revealed to me that the devil wants to shut my mouth, therefore I have to be careful when I speak but I should also be very concise and to the point. **Just because the devil takes it out of my**

mouth does not mean he can take it out of my soul.

What God gave me next was very empowering to me. I feel

that this word speaks to a lot of people that's why I have

shared it. There was a prophet in our church speaking to

people and giving them words of prophecy that God had

given him to share with them. (Of course this is an exciting

time for everyone in the church when God speaks, but

especially to a person who receives the Word.) It's easy for

me to be excited for somebody else, but when I start to

reflect on my own situation, I wonder when will God send

a word for me; have you forgotten about me your faithful

servant? Almost immediately God spoke to me and

reminded me of the story of Prodigal Son (*Luke 15:11-32*).

In this story the younger son leaves home and spends all he

has and then comes back home. His family is happy to see

him back and throws a big party for him. During all of this

the older son becomes upset because his father gives all of

95

his attention to the son that has come back home. The older

son makes the father aware of all he did for the son who

left and spent all of his money.

The older son had been at home with the father all of this

time and he indicated to his father that he never gave him a

party. The father answers his older son and says that he

never had to give him these things because all of these

things already belonged to him. So I say all of that to say,

hey you don't need to be prophesied to all of the time,

because you are the older son you have always been here

and God's going to take care of you. You must allow this

time for others who need to be inspired by His words and

prophecy so that they can come.

As a true Christian I have to step back and allow the sick to

see the "doctor" for their healing. **Remember that you**

already have access to it … just ask for it.

Until tomorrow, if it's the Lord's will

Gospel Professor

Day 15

Give and God will give it back to you. Whatever you need in life: love, joy, peace, etc., give that to someone else and God will give it to you 100 times more.

Everything is well in my soul today. It is day 15 of the 40-day fast. I have actually gained a pound, so I am at 267. I have however, been sick all day. This makes twice during this fast I have been sick or maybe I did not really get over it the first time. I am working on feeling better so I have spent a lot of time in bed today.

I was thinking that you, my blog audience, might become bored because I am writing less because of my sickness. Then I was reminded of the reason I was fasting and writing. It was not to be seen or heard, but to draw closer to God. So what if nobody ever reads any more entries? Should it matter? No, because this is my personal account of my 40-day experience with the King and I am sharing it with you. Therefore, I am refocused, and supremely confident in God that He is able to finish the work He has started in me.

This fast has so many parallels to our lives as humans. Not everyday is exciting and full of everything, but we do have days when things are hard. We have days when things are down and we have the exciting times also. They are all together in this perfect balancing act that God performs. **I believe we get these experiences in equal amounts like five days of joy, five days of sadness but God knows exactly how to place them so that we will not give up on this experience called: life.**

Believe it or not my walk with Christ is very much the same way. I have days when I feel that I can go to the graveyard and speak to dead bodies and I really believe they will come up out of the ground. Then I have those days that I feel like saying, "please let this be my last breath, I am so done with my life." Ever feel like that? I feel that sometimes people have this picture of Christians as these happy go lucky people all of the time, we are happy, and sometimes we are not. Yes in Christ I know I can do all things (*Philippians 4:13*) and I cast my worries on Him, therefore I don't have to worry (*Hebrews 12:1*).

That's the difference between us and everybody else. When these situations come -- and they do because it rains on the just as well as the unjust -- we have a Godly umbrella that we use to keep us from getting wet. That's why two people can be in the same situation and react to it totally different. It's raining around both of them but only one is getting wet.

So I ask you today: are you getting wet? Then get an

umbrella ... the covering of God.

Until tomorrow, if it's the Lord's will,

Gospel Professor

Day 16

Adam where are you? This is God's call to us today. Are you hiding among the trees because of sin, or are you in fellowship with God? So ask yourself, where am I?

I am thankful for life, health and strength. I am speaking those things as if they were. I am still sick but I am getting better. My weight today is down two pounds to 265. My energy levels are good and I'm feeling a lot better. I am a little down today because of all that is going on around me. The spirit of sickness was in the air.

I made a hospital visit today to visit my six-year-old cousin who is in the PICU. The situation is not looking good. I have not seen this boy since he was a very young infant. However, I have seen pictures of him since. I visited him shortly after surgery; the doctors heavily sedated him so that he would not injure himself further. He had somehow gotten a bacterial infection in his neck that is eating away at the flesh in his neck. It had started to eat away at his juggler vein and the doctors used surgery to clean it and tie off the vein so that it would not have further damage.

The worst part was that when I was leaving the room I shook the doctor's hand and he said that he was sorry. To me that was not a good sign from him. However, I have prayed about it and I look forward to writing you in the future about how God has miraculously healed his body. He is at the point only God can save him. His body has to fight off the infection on its own; surgery will not do any good at this point. *Lord send your healing power.*

While I was visiting my sick cousin God also used that as an opportunity for me to minister to others that needed to be restored. One of the ladies that was visiting him, I knew from my old church. We began to catch up since we had last seen each other. We then began to talk about the things of God and how she felt God calling her back to the church and how she missed the anointing of the Lord. I did my best to encourage her to come back and I do believe that she will at least visit us soon.

We have to be sensitive to God's spirit; we don't ever know when He will use a situation to push someone in the direction He wants them to go. This brings me to my last story of the day. As I was in the hospital talking to my cousin about his son I took him to get dinner and he began to tell me that I was different. I was not sure what he was talking about and he said, "I heard your conversation with that lady and you talk totally different than what I was used to hearing from you." I began to ask him in what ways am I talking different. He began to inform me that we need to talk much more than we have been. I was happy; I guess he sees something in me that he can glean from. I hope it's Jesus that he sees and I want him to get seriously rededicated back to the church. He has been blessed with so many talents and if he uses them for God's Glory he can

and will be blessed. So how are you using your talents?

I wonder, is God calling you and you are not listening? Or

are you not sure that it's God. Try the Holy Spirit like

Gideon did and answers the call *(Judges 6:36-39)*.

Until tomorrow, if it's the Lord's will,

Gospel Professor

Day 17

It's by grace through faith that we are saved, not by works. Salvation is a gift that has been given to us by God through Christ. It's up to us if we accept it.

When the sun is not shining in your area, be assured that it is shinning somewhere else. Today is day 17 of the 40-day fast and all is still well. I weigh 263 now, which is another two-pound loss as of today. I do not have much to say today, however I did have a good learning experience today with my Pastor. God also stretched me in another way today… I spent a significant amount of time with my Pastor today visiting the sick and praying for them. I have been to hospitals before to pray for people, but it was different this time. I was with my mentor and I was in learning mode. I carefully watched how he carried himself and interacted with the patients and their companions. He did not have to say much, but I did learn a lot. Learning from God is very much the same way, **He wants us to spend time with Him and we will learn from being in His presence.** The longer you are in His presence the more you learn and want to be like Him.

The most powerful and weakest position to be in is out of control of a situation. Really think about it like this. People are most fearful when they cannot control what is going to happen. People like control, we like to know the outcomes and many of us would even like to know the future. Being out of control is really a weak position to be in. You have to take whatever comes your way. At the same time this is the most powerful position to be in. Why? Because the Bible says when I am weak, that is when I am strong

(2 *Corinthians 12:10)*. When I am not in control, then God is in control. We must trust him to lead and guide us into all truth and understanding. We must have supreme confidence in him; he will never leave us nor forsake us. Do you feel

like giving Him control? How confident are you in His ability to take care of you? Do something interesting with your life and give God control right away.

It's clear that God only will do what we cannot do for ourselves; do your part and God will do what you can't do.

Until tomorrow, if it's the Lord's will,

Gospel Professor

Day 18

Words are the most powerful things in the universe. They are containers of power and things. We are justified or condemned by what we say. Speak life today.

Yes I am getting closer, to the halfway point of my 40-day fast. Today is day 18 of the fast and my weight is 263. Today has been up and down. However, I still give God the praise because He is worthy of all praise. I have a couple of good praise reports to share. By the way I have been tempted greatly to eat today but, God has been good to me and I am still holding on.

While getting ready this morning to go to work, God gave me a message for the next time that I preach. It was clear, as day and the message He gave me will reach all audiences. I had kind of been on a drought for a message but now I have two. I don't think people understand sometimes, that as a minister of Christ we have to fight for these messages, well at least I do.

I have to fight to get them and keep them until I at least write them down. Then even after that it's still tough to give it exactly how God has given it to you. It's almost like a mother wolf to the pups in her den. What a mother wolf does is first eat the food and then she vomits it back up after it has been somewhat digested so that the younger pups are able to eat it without being choked. I believe the process for ministers of the gospel is the same way. God gives us these messages and it's tough for us, as we have to live it and experience it.

After that we have to be able to tell you about the experience, much like this fast is for me. I am experiencing a lot of different things, but when I minister now I know what I have learned and digested will come out of me and bless others, because I allowed God to feed me.

God never ceases to amaze me. I wrote yesterday about how my young cousin was very sick and the doctors were giving up hope on him. I received a text message today that was telling me that the "Word was Doing the Work". In the message, I was informed that my little cousin's situation was starting to turn around. Yes in less than 24 hours his situation was starting to turn around. The antibiotics he was taking were starting to do their job and his body was responding to it positively. Thank You Jesus! I continue to pray and I want nothing short of a full recovery (if it's in God's will).

In all of this today, God provided another opportunity for me to minister. Ministry is much more than preaching on Sunday mornings. It's an all day, everyday thing to me. If you are serving people, then you are ministering to them.

I received another text from my little cousin's mother's sister. She asked if I would take her home. She had spent the last couple of days at the hospital with my sick cousin and needed to be relieved from being there. I was able to serve her and on the way home we had the most incredible conversation. God is really showing Himself strong in her life and I look forward to her visiting us at the church very soon, and becoming fully restored by God.

Lastly, tonight I wanted to speak about my dear friend. I think the world of this person; they really mean a lot to me and I consider them a great friend. However, this person was having some problems in their marriage like most people. The problems seemed to worsen as time passed, and things just seemed like they were not getting any better. While I was praying or typing the other night, God spoke to me to tell them to fast from meat for a couple of weeks. I asked them if this was a confirmation to what they already felt they needed to do? (Remember what I said earlier about prophecy -- it should only be a confirmation to what you already know.) They said yes and expressed to me that they were feeling inspired by my fasting anyway so they were looking forward to doing it.

What happened next was nothing short of amazing at least for this person. They started fasting and God started changing their situation around almost immediately. God started working on the other spouse because the fasting spouse finally decided to get out of the way and let God do it, by humbling themselves through fasting and prayer. To make a long story short, God shook the spouse's world and before it was all over, they were agreeing on things. The spouses were having positive communication and then they decided to fast and pray together. Wow! Tell me God isn't good and I will call you a liar every time.

The Bible says that the power of life and death are in the

tongue (Proverbs 18:21), so my question to you is simple:

Are you giving BIRTH or are you MURDERING today?

Until tomorrow, if it's the Lord's will,

Gospel Professor

Day 19

Everyday with Jesus is sweeter than the day before. God

has been good to me again today. Some may say how, and I

would say because He allowed me to wake up this morning

clothed in my right mind and strength in my body. What

else do you really need? My weight today is a steady 263; I

have not seen any significant changes there.

I went to work today and I had a pretty good day. The

students behaved themselves and it went off pretty much

without incident. This afternoon I spent a couple of hours

hunting and I was successful. The rest of my time was

spent fellowshipping with others from my church and

sharing different experiences.

As I reflect, I could not help but notice that after tonight I

will be at the half way point of this fast. I can look back

and see how far God has brought me. I never thought that I

would be able to fast this long. I have learned that: "I can do all things through Christ who strengthens me." The biggest thing about the second half of this fast is that I have to stay focused on why I am doing the fast. It is easy to lose focus because most of the things that I was seeking God for He has already done or is in the process of doing. So, why not quit, right?

But, I keep reminding myself that there are unseen bugs that need to be taken care of and the only way they can be gone forever is to complete the process. Remember whatever God starts in you He is able to finish and perform it in you. **Let God perform for you!**

Until tomorrow, if it's the Lord's will,

Gospel Professor

Day 20

When I think of the goodness of Jesus and all He has done

for me my soul cries out Hallelujah, I thank God for saving

me! Have you ever thought about all of the goodness of

Jesus and all of the things that He has done for you? I don't

know about you but it doesn't take much for me to think

about how many times He has spared my life, kept me from

danger, and made ways out of what seemed to be no way. I

have learned a lot during this first half of the fast and I am

continuing to learn how to have a perfect heart towards

God. Today is day 20 of the 40-day fast -- I really made it

twenty days without any food! I can't believe it. The verse

in the Bible that says, "As a man thinketh so is he,"

(*Proverbs 23:7*) really means more to me now because I am

living it. My weight today is still holding steady at 263.

I've been allowing myself to do things that are outside of what I would normally do. For example, I went to a chicken stew to fellowship with members from my church. Usually I would not attend an event like this not because there is something wrong but I was just out of my comfort zone.

Normally this type of thing is beyond my scope, it was cold outside and besides I was not eating. I was wondering why should I even go? When people saw me, many of them made comments about how they were shocked to see me there. I always considered myself to be a friendly and outgoing person. However, this made me realize that maybe I am only friendly in a certain way. I must be friendlier than that and also not have any prejudice in my heart at all. Maybe there was something in my heart that I did not know was there. Like anyone, I have my moments and I can be funny about certain things especially when it comes to my family. Then I thought about it, they are my family too. How many of us really count them as our family? Should I share the same moments with them as I would my blood family? Wait a minute, they are my blood family, we are all brought with a price and we share a common blood type the saving blood of Jesus.

My Pastor gave a powerful message today, and the most important part that I got out of it I want to share because it's truly worth repeating. He was talking about how God was looking for people with a perfect heart to bless. A perfect heart? How do you have one of those? I thought only Jesus had that kind of heart. The actual word here is: "friendly". So the question really is do you have a friendly heart? Are you a friend of God?

Do you embrace him on a daily basis? That's just it …

Jesus' heart was perfect because He was friendly to all of

us. How friendly are we to everyone else? Be friendly

today and you will never want tomorrow.

Until tomorrow, if it's the Lord's will,

Gospel Professor

Section 3

Pushing

Praying Until Something Happens Invoking New Grace

DAY

21 of 40

Day 21

Blessed is the man who puts his trust in the Lord. Today when the enemy tries to bring doubt, just know this one thing: you're blessed because you trust God!

It is official, I am past the halfway point and I can see a little light at the end of the tunnel. My weight today is 261. My fast is going well, yes I do still have my trying times, but overall everything is good. I finally have my mind under control -- somewhat. What I mean is that I am not having those thoughts that tell me it's time for me to eat all of the time.

I struggled today with other things. I promised to be honest with you and I will. I did not struggle with food today, but I had other struggles. Most would believe that food is the only struggle that you will have during a fast; however I struggled with my eyes today. Yes, like most men I do have to make a daily covenant with my eyes, but it was unusually tough today for some reason. I found my mind wondering a lot. This can be dangerous because sin starts as a thought and once that thought is fully conceived then it can become an action.

It can be especially hard with certain work environments to keep your eyes covered. I work at a college and most of the girls there are half-dressed 85% of the time. It does not matter if the weather is warm or cold. After a while I had just become numb to it because you see it so much. Today I was not; I guess the devil figured that I have this hunger thing down so he is trying to hit me with his next best weapon. The Bible tells me that, "**No weapon formed against me shall prosper**" *(Isaiah 54:17)*. I will get through it. I just have to stay focused and stay prayed up. It's amazing that during this fast things that you thought were dead are brought back to you. God knows exactly what you need to work on and has His way of bringing them up.

Lastly, God has been bringing a lot of old friends and people I used to associate with back into my life. It seems odd at times but when we start talking I find out quickly why we have crossed paths again. God is allowing me to mend broken fences and to ask for forgiveness for my past wrongs. He is also teaching me lessons from these relationships and allow those people to see me in a new light. God never ceases to amaze me. He is fixing things in my past and giving closure to situations that have caused pain and hurt. By fixing these situations it is enabling me to be whole. By being whole it enables me to help others to become whole. So, are you whole? What is keeping you from becoming whole?

Pushing:

Praying Until Something Happens Invoking New Grace

What do you do when doubt shows its ugly head? Do you

still trust God? How much do you really trust Him?

Until tomorrow, if it's the Lord's will,

Gospel Professor

Day 22

To whom much is given, much is required. We ask for a great deal, but are we ready for the requirements? Are we prepared for the blessing? God is ready, are you?

Today is a great day to be alive. My weight has been steady today at 261, and I am very tired. I made some bad choices and now I am paying for it with my body. I decided last night to stay up a lot later than I normally do talking to an old friend. As I was talking earlier I was still mending fences. By the time I decided I should quit for the night it was 2 a.m. So that was not that bad, but what made it bad was that I had to rise early the next day to drive students in my program to a field trip. It was brutal because I was so tired.

The field trip today was to the North Carolina State Fair. It was brutal at times but I held on to my integrity and did not eat anything. It was hard because the fair is just an open

market for food. That's pretty much what you go for; at

least that's what I used to do. I felt like I was walking

through Hell with gasoline boots on and made it out

untouched. I thank God for keeping me so focused to make

it out. He means so much to me that the temporary pleasure

of food will not keep me away from Him.

After coming back from the fair I had practice for the

church play that I am participating in and had a swell time.

Earlier in these blogs I was referring a lot to God stretching

me, and now I am starting to see the fruits of that. I am now

doing things that are out of my norm and I am enjoying it. I

am finding new things and finding that many of them are a

natural fit for me. I would have never explored this option

if it were not for this fast. I am birthing the new things that

God has given me. This leads me to ask, "What are you

doing differently these days? Do you see a need for a change? Are you willing to birth that change?"

This is one of the codes that I live by, because God has given me a lot. So what are you doing with what you were given? Are you using it for His glory?

Until tomorrow, if it's the Lord's will,

Gospel Professor

Day 23

The message of the Cross is foolishness to those who are

perishing, but it is the MESSAGE. The closer the Cross,

the thinner the crowd; there is room at the Cross.

How can I say goodbye to what I used to be and welcome

in what I am becoming? That is the question that I am

constantly asking myself these days. I know that God has a

lot in store for me but how do you handle it all? When will

it happen? Will I be ready? When will the ultimate plan

come all together for me? I know I just have to hold out

and in due season I will reap the harvest. My weight today

was 259, which is down 2 lbs from the previous day.

Today I am starting to deal with hunger pains again … they

have returned. On the third day of the fast my hunger pains

all but disappeared but sad to say they have resurfaced and

are a beast to deal with. The way I make it through is by

telling myself that my hunger in temporal but my gain from this fast is eternal. You know what; it really is an eternal gift.

The Bible says that obedience is better than sacrifice (*1 Samuel 15:22*). So I asked myself the question, "What does it mean to be obedient by sacrificing? God the father was obedient by sacrificing Himself for us. He did not want to do it; we have evidence of that in the garden of Gethsemane when He asked that this cup be taken away from Him (*Matthew 26:39*). The cup He was talking about was sin and death that He was going to consume on our behalf. By being obedient He sacrificed Himself. If you really think about it: being obedient is a sacrifice because you are laying down what you possibly wanted to do in order to follow the command that was given.

Living for God is not that tough if you have a made-up mind to live for Him. However, the problem comes in for us, as a human is that we cannot keep our mind made up to live for him. You ask how is this possible? Well, we live in a body that constantly has to fight the evil things of this world. Sometimes as Christians we lose those battles and sometimes we win them. **I believe as a believer that we will win all of our battles if we call upon the name of God.** The problems come from us not using the power of God in all of our battles. For some reason we limit God, to be a man of ancient history and not the living God of today. Take Jesus out of the box and live a new life with him today.

Until tomorrow, if it's the Lord's will,

Gospel Professor

Day 24

It is easy to call men great, and it is easy to say that men are gifted because God uses them. But can their character keep them where God takes them?

Day 24 of the 40-day fast has come and gone, my weight went back up to 261; I must be bloated for some reason. I admit I have started to get lazy when it comes to writing these blogs. However, I will push myself through these rough spots. Like anything else after you do it for a while you can become complacent. That is the point when you must really focus and push forward, you have to be more than a starter you also want to be a finisher (*Mark 13:13*). I would be the first to admit that I have been a good starter but not always a good finisher. I have been asking the Lord to help me to finish things.

To put this more in perspective, take this example: A person who wants to lose 20 pounds, and they put themselves on a low calorie diet. The first couple of days are good and they've lost about a pound. About two more weeks go by and the person loses one pound. Then, three more weeks go by and the person only loses one pound. At this point they become frustrated, quit, or lose confidence in the process. I have seen this many times because I have done it. Well, a couple of things can be learned here: you learn to evaluate yourself, and determine if you are really sticking to your plan. Why is your plan not working? Was the plan a very good one to start with? Was the plan realistic? Next, you learn to check your commitment. How committed are you? How bad do you want it? Is it really worth the effort? These are the types of questions you should ask yourself when you look at goals and things that you want to accomplish in your life. For me, I have always prided myself on: "Working smarter not harder." I also suggest it to you -- having a solid plan helps to make you a finisher.

Another example would be this book you are reading now. The seed of writing a book was planted in me long ago. I always wonder when and how I would get this accomplished; then while on this fast (the fast you have been reading about). God gave me the plan; it was a plan to work smarter not harder when writing. So for the longest time I had this plan to just sit down and write until I was just empty. Guess what happened? I never found the time to write and I was always empty it seemed. Then God laid on my heart to share my real experiences with you through a daily writing and that writing turned into chapters, sections and behold a book. **That's how God works -- from thought to action to fulfillment**.

The last thing I would like to share with you today is about happiness. God has truly in the last couple of weeks really taught me what true happiness really is. I was amazed by the revelation and I want to share it with you. I must give you the disclaimer that true happiness is an experience and not just a feeling. It is an experience like getting filled with the Holy Ghost or Holy Spirit.

True happiness can in my opinion only be experienced when you are truly happy for someone else. Think about it for a moment. You cannot be happy for someone else when you are not happy yourself. By nature we as humans are selfish. Wanting the best for yourself is nothing to be ashamed of. However, to really rejoice with somebody else for what they receive, takes a person who is secure in who they are and what they are capable of doing and knows their place in God. Then it's easy to be happy for somebody else because you know what he or she has does not belong to you. The exciting part about it is that you are now more able to realize when things are *for you* because you are sure

of the things that are *not for you*. Think about it.

Another thing I thought about was that we all have our

struggles with character from time to time. When God

allows us to go through things like failure and pain, He is

building character in us that will allow us to stay in the

places that He wants to take us. That is why I believe it,

when the Bible says, "promotion comes from God"

(Psalms 75:6-7). This is because only He truly knows if we

are qualified to go to the next level. Our outward

appearance to people can say that we are ready but our

character can be screaming out, "No, I can't go!" Would

you want to be there and not stay there? In our society

today we see many self-promoted people. When it comes to

this, I recall the lessons from my childhood when my father

would tell me that the same people who put you up there

are the same ones who will take you down. Another thing

he would tell me is if you pay your dues now, you will

know how to stay there when you get there and how to treat

people. **My advice to you would be to let God promote**

you and you'll be ready when He pulls your resume.

Until tomorrow, if it's the Lord's will,

Gospel Professor

Day 25

God is better to me than I will ever be to myself. My weight today is 258; down about three pounds. Today marks day 25 of my 40-day fast. I have fifteen more days to go. As I am writing tonight, I sit back and reflect on my day. My day was cool but something kind of crazy happened to me today. I learned a valuable lesson today. I will soon explain what happened … the test came first and the lesson later and I failed miserably. I understand that life is 10% what happens to me and 90% how I react to it and I did not react very well.

I had a pretty good day and I left work early to lend a hand to my friend that has just purchased a new home. While on the way to his house, I was driving on the highway and the car next to me began to drift over into my lane and I blew the horn to notify the driver.

Pushing:

Praying Until Something Happens Invoking New Grace

The driver was on the cell phone and looked up at me and put his middle finger in the air and began saying something. This of course pissed me off! All I was doing was protecting him and myself from being hit, but I guess he did not see it that way. So I pulled up and was looking at him like, "What's up with that."? He began to stick his middle finger back at me, while sill talking. By this time I am enraged and I started talking back. Then the driver of the other car swerved his car in front of me. I was even madder than before because now he was trying to kill me. At this point I pulled up beside the driver and told him to pull over. I am thinking I am going to beat the crap out of this guy.

Needless to say I did not get my hands on the guy because after I told him to pull over he ran off at an even higher speed to get away. I thought about the encounter. What if this guy was crazy? Why did I react to the guy the way I did? Why did I get so upset toward the guy? Now that I

thought about it, this guy could have killed me over

something that was senseless as him sticking his middle

finger at me. The reason I got angry was because I could

not control the situation. Think about it; when are you

really upset? Are you upset at the thing or are you upset

because you cannot control the situation? What you will

find is if you get to the heart of the issue -- control is really

the issue. We all want to always be in control, but what

happens when we cannot be? Do we become upset or do

we trust God? What I learned today was even in little

situations like that I should have trusted God to take care of

it.

Like most people, I want to be in control, but I learned that

the more I want to be in control the more I should let it go.

I don't always know what's best for me, but He knows and

Pushing:

Praying Until Something Happens Invoking New Grace

I have to give him total control of my life. So **I have learned to react by allowing Him to lead.**

I trust that God will change me and He will change the things that I cannot change if I give up control to Him. **He will make things better for me or change the things around me to work for me.**

Until tomorrow, if it's the Lord's will,

Gospel Professor

Day 26

The Bible says, "Raise up a child in the way they should go
and when they are old they shall not depart from it"
(Proverbs 22:6). Children are often viewed as a gift from the
Lord, but what about good parents? I have been fortunate to
be blessed with two good parents. I don't think that parents
get their due, at least the good ones. Each parent has their
niche, and they know their strengths, which make them
great together.

Today I was able to spend the whole day with my parents.
They come into town to spend time with my wife and I at
least once a year. My parents together gave life to five
children. Through prayer, diligence, sacrifice and hard
work they raised five college graduates. Yes, all five of
their children attended and finished college. I find this to be
a great feat for any family, especially African American.

Pushing:

Praying Until Something Happens Invoking New Grace

Today I realized how important it is to have great parent role models in your life. If the Lord would not have blessed me with such great parents as part of His plan for me, I truly don't know how I would have turned out. My parents are not perfect and yes I have seen them make mistakes, but to see how they handle the setbacks and move forward, is a lesson in itself.

As God's children, He has been the ultimate role model for us. He has shown us through His life, that we can make it and not lose our soul or integrity in the process. God made the ultimate sacrifice by giving His Son to us. This would be the same as a parent giving their last. It's not always easy to do the right thing when the wrong thing makes itself a viable option. However, we must strive to make better decisions and live our lives on such a level that the world sees the difference. I call it living life in *High Definition* (HD).

Pushing:

Praying Until Something Happens Invoking New Grace

Anyone who has watched a standard TV and then an HD TV can clearly see the difference in the two. Make no mistake about it, the clarity of an HD TV is desired if it is possible because you can see more detail. The more detail you see the more you can enjoy the show and gather the information that you are seeking. The standard TV just does not do that. With that said I ask the question, which is easier for a person seeking God (sinner) for a better life to see? Do you want to be seen as living the standard life or do you want to be seen in High Definition? Do you want your walk to be seen fuzzy or clearly? I don't know about you but I want to be seen clearly, with clarity, so that you know exactly who I am and whom I belong to.

We learn from each other and if you are living in HD, I can learn from your mistakes and you can learn from mine. **The Bible says that, "Iron sharpens iron"** *(Proverbs 27:17).* **So let's all live on an HD level so that our walk and purpose is seen clearly."**

Until tomorrow, if it's the Lord's will,

Gospel Professor

Day 27

Day 27 of my 40 day fast is now complete. My weight today is 257 and holding. Is God happy with my praise? That's the question that I ask myself from time to time. I sometimes wonder if I am pleasing in His sight. Have you ever thought about that? Sometimes in life we wonder if we are pleasing to Him when things come against us. We wonder if we are in sin or what have we done. You often hear people ask the question: "Why do bad things happen to good people?" To be honest with you nobody on this earth really knows the answer to that question. God and He alone holds the answer to that question. All we can do is trust His word that, "All things work together for the good of them that love the Lord" *(Romans 8:28)*.

Many bad things happened to Job and the Bible says he did not sin *(Job 2:10)*. It was God allowing him to be tested. How many times are we being tested by God and we blame the devil and circumstances? I am finding out more and more each day that I alone am my worst enemy. Often the things that I do are self-inflicted wounds in my thinking, character, and self-discipline. I cannot be as successful as God wants me to be until I am satisfied within myself with the gifts and talents that God has given me. It's a constant struggle within yourself, trying to realize that God chose you to do His will. However God makes you worthy through His Spirit. I am still fighting at times when I am down about past sins. Yes, things in your past can affect your future, but finding the power to get over them is hard.

Every time I think like this I create a self-inflicted wound. I have to stop killing myself, can you relate? Do you do self-destructive things? Not physically, but mentally? God gives us a choice to renew our mind.

Another thing that happened is that God chastised me today and I was wondering why. Then he gave me a revelation.

149

Pushing:

Praying Until Something Happens Invoking New Grace

One of my problems is that the fast, over the last couple of weeks, has become easy to me -- a lifestyle and not a sacrifice. I still need to work on some things. If I am going to go deeper I need to go stricter. Therefore, I will only drink water and take vitamins for the next seven days (no more fruit juices or Boost). I will admit my fasting and giving have been consistent but my prayer life has suffered. My two-strain cord is great, but what if I can get my prayer life as consistent as my fasting and giving? I've got to do better and I will do better.

Character

I was watching one of my favorite websites (www.youtube.com) and I was listening to TD Jakes speak on the subject of "Saul's Suicide". It was one of the most powerful messages that I have ever heard. I could not help but see myself in the story of King Saul. I felt so bad because I believe Saul and I share a lot of character traits. I believe it was destiny for me to come across this message. In this message, TD Jakes gave seven character traits about Saul that led to his downfall and self-inflicted wounds. I've decided that for the next seven days I will concentrate on one trait each day to work on. I will work on each one everyday, but I will put special emphasis on a particular one each day. I want to be perfected in Jesus because I may be morally good -- but my character is not. What about you? How is your character?

The seven character traits are:

1. Disobedience (i.e.: Not following what God tells you to do)

2. Arrogance (i.e.: thinking more highly than you ought)

3. Rebellion (i.e.: purposely doing wrong things)

4. Denial (i.e.: not realizing faults)

5. Repentance (i.e.: I'm sorry)

Pushing:

Praying Until Something Happens Invoking New Grace

6. Ego (i.e.: your image)

7. Murder (i.e.: not killing what needs to die)

Some of you *suffer* from these traits also. So be honest with yourself and ask… How is my character?

Take heed and work toward perfection -- don't interview well and work horribly.

Until tomorrow, if it's the Lord's will,

Gospel Professor

Day 28

It is useless to give offerings to God while you are at odds with your brother. Before you come to God, go to your brother and be reconciled. Reconcile today!

Disobedience is the refusal to obey. My focus today was disobedience, so I have given it serious thought. I've asked myself, in what ways have I been disobedient? Some things are easy to identify in my life like not following things in the Bible. What about the things that God tells you to do directly? These are the things that I struggle with the most. The first step to being obedient is to understand the command and whom the command is from. I admit sometimes I miss the voice of God. My hearing is not always clear. That is because sometimes my judgment can be clouded.

Pushing:

Praying Until Something Happens Invoking New Grace

We all have times when our judgment is clouded. The only way I am sure when God is speaking to me is through prayer. I often have various thoughts floating through my mind, some good and some bad. Some of these thoughts I feel like they come from God but sometimes I am not sure, because I am not as in touch with Him as I should be.

I have learned **in order to be able to be obedient you have to place yourself in a position to listen**. I have found this position for me to be on my knees. This does not mean that I am praying but I have put myself in a quiet place to hear from God. God cannot speak unless you allow Him to.

My day was pretty good. God allowed me to minister today in a couple of different ways. I was first able to minister to others in my office about the transfer of spirits. The question was asked about the transfer of spirits and I took the opportunity to explain and minister. Another opportunity came my way via a question on the website

Facebook.com. I was able to answer a couple of questions there.

The most exciting ministry of the day came at the rest home that I was able to visit. On a couple of Monday nights out of the month I participate in the rest home ministry at my church. Tonight we were able to minister to those who are not able to help themselves. We were able to sing God's praises and share the Word of God with them. We also prayed with the residents that were there.

I have to tell you about one resident in particular that was there tonight. When we first got there a certain lady kept asking me to pray for her. I told the lady that I would pray for her at the end of the service. When the end of the service came we were all praying together and this lady asked me to pray for her again. So this time I begin to pray for her as she sat down. I was about twenty-five seconds into my prayer with her and the lady immediately jumped up and ran out of the door.

Everybody in the prayer circle was looking at me and afterward asked me what did I do to her? I explained that all I did was pray for her but I was speaking directly in her ear. Now what seemed weird about this was that the lady begged for me to pray for her but as soon as I started to pray for her she took off. Well, I would like to believe that her spirit was quickened and the power of God touched her, but to be honest I am not sure. It was truly an awkward moment regardless of what it was.

Tomorrow's focus will be arrogance. I will meditate on that all day along while listening to God's voice. By the way my weight today was 256, down one pound.

Until tomorrow, if it's the Lord's will,

Gospel Professor

Day 29

The focus of my fast today was working on arrogance. There is a fine line between being confident and being arrogant. I know that I sometimes walk this line. However, I do want to be confident. I have learned that being confident is a good thing, but when you use that confidence to boost yourself passed where you are then that's when the problem occurs. What we must realize is that anything that gives more glory to ourselves than God is dangerous. In the Bible, God says that, "No flesh shall glory in My sight" *(Roman 3:20).* If you are arrogant, you place what you know and who you are above God. Nothing in our lives should be above God.

My fast has been well today. This is my second day drinking nothing but water. It has been a challenge sometimes but I have found the inner strength to manage.

Pushing:

Praying Until Something Happens Invoking New Grace

My weight today is 256, which is the same as it was yesterday.

Have you ever really stopped to think about how others view you versus how you view yourself? I have been thinking about this very thing a lot lately. I have had so many people come up to me lately and tell me how much they admire me. If you only knew, I don't see myself they way others do. I do believe that's a good thing. Why? Because if I saw myself the way others see me I would be full of pride. Pride is a dangerous thing because it gives you a false sense of self. Only you know what you would be without the mercy of God. I guess that is how I look at myself. I clearly understand that we are all one mistake away from being in a totally different situation. I understand not to take life and what I have for granted. That's why I try to live everyday to the fullest because you don't know when your time could be up.

Pushing:

Praying Until Something Happens Invoking New Grace

I am learning more and more each day to give of myself in ways that stretch me. **God runs our cup over so that others may have a drink from His saucer.**

Until tomorrow, if it's the Lord's will,

Gospel Professor

Day 30

No matter what, rejoice. No matter how you feel, rejoice. No matter what they said, rejoice. No matter what they did, rejoice. Theme for today: REJOICE ANYWAY!

Today is day 30 out of 40 and my focus was on the rebellion characteristic. I did not focus on it as much as I would have liked to. However, I really do believe that the purpose of reviewing each one of these characteristics is for me to do an internal review of who I am. Rebellion to me is a wiliness to go against an order or a direct command from leadership. My trouble with rebellion to me is justified. I have a problem following people whom I don't believe they know what they are doing or saying. In that case, I guess you can call it a lack of faith in a person or individual.

Pushing:

Praying Until Something Happens Invoking New Grace

What I am realizing is that I should trust God and follow after Him. I can't help but hold the thoughts in the back of my mind, thinking what if they are leading us wrong. I guess this has been unintentionally planted into me because I have been around leadership who have abused their authority. This makes me think: can you ever be justified for being rebellious? Can the same be said about being disobedient? I have seen good people get messed up behind being 100% obedient to bad leadership. Well, what I have found out is that if you are under bad leadership and God reveals this to you, you immediately change your situation. I would cautiously say that sometimes we make things worse and we use it as an excuse to leave a situation.

I was so hooked on my tradition and religious views that I was much like a woman that is in an abusive relationship. You realize that love doesn't hurt and you should not be getting beaten up and broken inside of the hospital, or in this case, the church.

I don't know about you but I am rejoicing. I never thought that I would make it this far. God has truly taught me some things on this journey. Wow ... 30 straight days of fasting and my soul rejoices in the Lord! My weight today was 254 which means I am down another two lbs. I must admit I have nine more days to go and I'm a bit weary and weak in body. My soul is good; I am drawing near to the mountaintop.

I heard TD Jakes say once, that the closer you get to the top of the mountain the smaller your circle becomes. The mountain gets smaller as you begin to climb. I can see an end and the birth in sight, can you?

Until tomorrow, if it's the Lords will,

Gospel Professor

Section 4

The Birth:

Bringing In Relief Through Humility

Day 31

Yes I am feeling great, but I cannot deny the hunger that I have. Since I have been fasting stricter this week it has been a beast. I have lost another two lbs. today so I am down to 252 and its day 31 of the 40-day fast. Denial was the characteristic that I focused on today. Denial is one of those gateway characteristics.

Denial is a gateway because if you don't recognize what is going on, how can you fix it? There is nothing more frustrating for those around you than to know that a problem exists for you, however they know you don't want to face the truth. There are certain things in all of our lives that we just have to face. If we keep denying the problem or situation we miss the opportunities to grow and conquer the problem or situation. Denial is a strong characteristic because it never allows you passed the starting point. Getting help for someone who is in denial is impossible.

Even in rehab facilities they tell you that the first step is to admit your problems. The reason they do this is so that they can crush denial and get the person to come to terms with their problem(s).

Do you have things in your life that you are denial about? Are you in denial about your feelings, your health, your walk with Christ? Now is time to confront those things that you are in denial about. One of the hardest things for me to do is to admit when I am wrong. I like to be right and in my mind I usually am, however I also really know this is not always true. One of the hardest things for me to do is to admit when I am wrong. When I think of denial I think about tragic events. For example, if someone has a friend that is injured in a wreck. Once the other friend finds out, they usually state, "I can't believe it…" or they will not believe it until they are provided with evidence of the event. Even then, some still do not believe it. The first step to dealing with that situation is realizing that the friend is hurt and start to do things that would help in their recovery. If you do not do this you will not be any help to the person and you may become an obstacle more than a help.

During this fast there are several things in my spirit I have been in denial about. I have decided to confront these things. Things such as jealousy, anger and procrastination had kept me from being everything that God desires me to be. So I admit, yes I have a jealously problem in some areas of my life now I must create steps to deal with it. However, I have taken step one. I admit that I have anger issues at times when I feel that I cannot control a situation. **I like to feel in control of my situation and when I decided to tell God my plans He laughed at me.** That tells you what He thought about my plans.

My life is not my own I am bought with a price. Therefore when things do not go the way I expect, then I do not need to get angry, but realize that I am following God's plan. His plan has my best interest in mind. I admit that I am a

167

procrastinator. God has given me an awesome ability but I have this thing of waiting to the last minute to do things. If I don't wait until the last minute to do things, then I can do them better, with less frustration and more quality.

So now it's your turn. What things are you in denial about that needs cleaning up in your life? Make your own list and address each one. Then create a plan of action to deal with each one. **You have always had the ability but now you have the way.**

Who would have ever thought that growing up spiritually is as hard if not harder than growing up physically?

Until tomorrow, if it's the Lord's will,

Gospel Professor

Day 32

Moses spent 40 years in the desert that he would eventually lead Israel through. Where you are now is simply a training ground you'll one day lead others through.

Day 32 of the 40 day fast is here. Wow! Believe it or not I really don't miss the food that bad. It's just when I am around people and can smell it that makes it tough for me. I lost another two lbs. today and my weight is an even 250. That's cool but it's really not about losing weight but getting closer to the Father. However, I am still dealing with my character.

As I thought today, I realized that my skill set, my look, my way of talking -- pretty much everything about me -- says I am ready to go to the next level. All accept my character. Now to some people the character issues that I feel I have are minimal but it's a big deal to me. No, I don't want to be perfect but I want to be as close to it as possible. Why? The reason is simple once I am promoted to the next level I want to be able to stay there.

An example would be a person who is exercising to lose weight. They run five miles every morning to help aid in the process of losing weight. That's great but as soon as they are finished running they go home and consume a large pepperoni pizza. Now that is counterproductive. Running five miles is hard work so you expect to see results of their labor, but you notice on the scale that you've have gained five pounds. There is a lesson to be learned here. All of the pieces must work together at the same time doing their job to ensure success. If not, you are spinning your wheels. When you are doing the right thing, but also doing bad things to cancel out your good things you do not go anywhere. You become frustrated with all of the good you did and it was easier to do the bad.

I see this so often with Christians and others striving to do better in Christ. We do some things well but the things that we do not do well overtake us and stain our gifts. Therefore we quit the church, or worse lose faith. An example of this in the church is a person whom God has blessed with the gift of song. (Remember that gifts are giving without repentance so if you've got it you've got it.) This person sings the church down on Sunday morning but the night before they were getting drunk and was involved in fornication. **Sin, when it pays its wage, pays in death.** Yes, not only are you killing your gift and spirit, but once sin has taken its course your final payment will be death (*Romans 6:23*).

That point now brings me to the characteristic that I was to focus on today -- which was repentance. Repentance in theory seems easy enough, however very few of us truly repent, me included. True repentance is to ask God for forgiveness and once He grants that forgiveness you are <u>not</u>

to make the same transgression again. Using that definition, how many of us really repent? Without a doubt I struggle with this. There are some things that I have repented from and have never made that transgression again. However, there are those other things that I find myself repenting daily for. Of course I am trying to get to the point where it's not an issue anymore and I do believe I will get there, but if I don't, I rely on grace and mercy to see me through.

Grace and mercy are only applied to the truly sincere. God knows your intentions and He knows the things that you struggle with, but do not use it as a crutch to do wrong, because He knows that too. As a believer, I would feel safe in saying that I probably have repented several thousands of times and if I live long enough, that number will probably be in the zillions. The most important part is that we can repent and that God is just to forgive us for those sins. So don't take grace and mercy for granted, but use them with the same diligence that you would with your own life. After all He gave His life so that we might have life and have it more abundantly (John 10:10).

Until tomorrow, if it's the Lord's will,

Gospel Professor

Day 33

Getting closer ... today is day 33 of the 40-day fast. I have gone 33 consecutive days without eating anything. This fast continues to be a life changing experience for me, and how I view the various situations around me.

My character focus for today was the dreaded ... "EGO".

Ego, simply put, is how importantly you view yourself. How do you view yourself? Have you ever thought about it? I often think about it. I have had my share of problems in this area. I have suffered with the "ME" syndrome -- when you view yourself as a victim of every situation and nothing good happens to you.

Everything that goes on is never my fault and the world revolves around me. Therefore if you don't do what I say it makes me upset because I don't have control and it irritates me. Have you ever been there? Trust me I know that I am not alone.

Sometimes dealing with your personal ego is really tough because it causes you to take an evaluative look at yourself. **Most people are scared to spend time with themselves because it causes you to deal with yourself.**

Once you start to deal with your inner issues you soon realize that you are <u>not</u> the sun and the world does <u>not</u> revolve around you.

You start to see your issues and how you should deal with them. Most importantly you understand that tests and trials come to make you stronger and to help prepare you for situations of life that may arise.

Until tomorrow, if it's the Lord's will,

Gospel Professor

Day 34

Day 34 of the 40-day fast, I have not had anything to eat for 34 days to put this into perspective I have not eaten anything the entire month of October. Well today, after praying and listening to my body, I have decided that, the last seven days of the fast will be a Daniel fast. With this, I will consume veggies and some choice bread, but no meats. This has been an incredible journey. God has really blessed me through this fast. I have decided to switch over to a Daniel fast for the last seven days; I will explain why. I was not fasting for weight loss or to harm my body. The weight loss was good, trust me I needed it, but I was at a point that I was starting to harm my body and developing a case of jaundice. I felt that the time had come to make the switch.

Today I spent a great deal of time in reflection. I went from barely being able to fast one day to being able to go a little over one month. The things that I wrote about in the beginning that I wanted God to address, He either addressed or He changed the color lens that I look through, and changed me. Some would say that this fast was not a success because I only did 33 consecutive days without food, but God reminded me that I was doing it to get closer to Him and not to boast in myself. See, I realized that if I would have made it I might have boasted in myself. However, stopping at this point helps me to understand that I have come far but I can only go where God's will allows me to go.

I have learned that timing in my season is essential to what God has called me to do. I can't get ahead of God. He knows my dedication to Him, and how much I am chasing after His heart. And like the tower of Babel He knew that I had the will and the means to complete the fast but He allowed circumstances – my jaundice to happen for His perfect timing.

I understand more and more each day that God's will is perfect and all of the imperfect things that you and I do are perfectly already included in His plan.

If God allows my gift to manifest itself before its time, something that is good when used properly can be deadly because it was used before its time. Take, for example, a child being given a loaded gun. The child does not understand or know the potential of the thing that they have in their hand. They have the power to end life, protect life, intimidate and command authority. Everyone around them knows that they possess this power because they see the loaded gun, but they are scared to deal with the child because they don't know how the child would handle the great power they have. Will he use the power to kill himself, to kill others, or protect others?

That is the danger that others see in people through the spiritual and natural world of those with talents and God-given gifts. They are afraid of what they could do. They don't know if you will kill them, protect them, or just abuse your authority. That is a powerful thing. Could this person be you? What will you do with that power, that revelation, that talent, that authority?

A lot of us, including myself, are 'babies that have guns'. Many of us know that we are not yet mature enough in God to be able to use our guns properly and to the full capacity of their use. However, they (Pastors, Elders, other people of God) want to show us how to use our guns and once they are sure of our ability to use them properly God issues them bullets to give us that "only fit our gun". **The training fits everybody, but the bullets issued to you are only for you and there are certain things in this life that God has put you here to begin or end.** It's your silver bullet that will cause that certain demon enemy to fall. As more and more of us discover that we are just in training of how to use the weapon but not the owners, then we will progress forward. Meaning that I let you do what God has called you to do and not interfere.

I say all of this to say that there are things that need to be murdered in all of us.

God has given us the ability to do this. However, we must endure and learn from sound teaching from Godly teachers. **We must submit ourselves to sound doctrine so that we won't murder the part of us that God desires to use** *(Titus 1:9).*

Until tomorrow, if it's the Lord's will,

Gospel Professor

Day 35

Created in the image of God, WOW! Did you hear that!!

God's DNA is in us! Now tell me again, what can't you

do, overcome, or defeat? Who's your Daddy!!

Can you say relief? Whoa! Yes today is day 35 of the 40-day fast, but now I am still Daniel fasting the rest of the way. I ate for the first time in 34 days and my body responded well. I am pleasantly pleased with some of the new eating habits that I will employ. I have learned a lot of discipline along the way. I am just thankful to God for sparing my life and allowing me to be able to enjoy the great things that this side of Glory has to offer.

I am also learning how to be content in life. This is a tough lesson for somebody like me. I am very outgoing and I like to do everything. I felt that I was not living life unless my plate was running over with things to do. I have been learning through this process that it's okay to have one thing on my plate and do it so well that nobody else wants to do it because you do it so well. It feels really good to do something so well that your contribution to the task is needed.

I also learned that to be the ultimate person at doing a task means to train somebody else on how to do the task. Why? If you can teach the task to someone else it shows that you have mastery; it also helps you to live through the task. The person you teach will inherit the same task skills and spirit of excellence that you posses. Then this person will pass it to the next and on and on.

So if you are really the best at what you do, then teach someone else and your legacy will take care of itself. **Be the best and God will do the rest.**

Until tomorrow, if it's the Lord's will,

Gospel Professor

Day 36

Let's just get through today; tomorrow has enough of worry of its own. Seek today the Kingdom of God and God will take care of tomorrow, just like He did today.

Day 36 of the 40-day fast. Have you ever wondered how different your life would be if you were 100% obedient to God 100% of the time. Okay, I know what you are thinking, that would be impossible. Really think about it for a moment. Has God ever told you to do something and you hesitated, and it caused you to miss out on an opportunity to do something great for Him? I think about things like this from time to time. I go over the reasons in my mind of why I was not obedient to Him in that exact moment. The reasons are numerous.

What I am learning is that learning to be 100% obedient is the process of growing from "Milk 2 Meat". You have to learn God's voice and be obedient. It is not easy and sometimes it's embarrassing. I have had some

183

bouts with doing what God has told me to do. People tell me all of the time how they admired how I just moved when God tells me to move. As they lift me up I tear myself down as quickly as they lift. Why? I can't help but think of all of the times that I did not listen or did not move. I remember the hesitation, fear and fear of embarrassment on my part.

I have a couple of instances that I will share with you that have been deeply personal to me and the lessons that I have learned from them have been life changing. These were intimate moments that I had with God, and through these experiences I now understand why Paul said that I would be a fool for Christ *(2 Corinthians 11:23)*.

It's hard for me to tell you this but this is a true story about my experience of learning God's voice and what I gained from it. Once God spoke to me clearly and told me to pray for a man that I knew very little about. I felt a strong impression on my heart to pray for him. I did from a distance, but God had a unusual request for me ... He told

me to pray for the man's testicles.

Now, I usually lay hands on people when I pray if I feel led

to do so, but that was not the problem. Needless to say I

was very, very uncomfortable with this request because I

barely knew the man and he barely knew me, and of

course, 'real men' just don't do things like that. I struggled

with the request so much that I did not do it the first time,

or the second, or the third. You can't run from what God

wants you to do. Yes, I was Jonah for a while and I was

working on getting swallowed up by disobedience *(Jonah*

1:3). It came to a point that God allowed it to consume me

in prayer. Every time I prayed it would come to mind.

Every time I saw him it came to mind. Eventually it got to a

point that I could not take it anymore. The next time I saw

the gentleman I asked if I could pray for him and I told him

what God wanted me to do. To my amazement that guy did

not reject so I asked him to hold himself in that area and I put my hand over his hand and began to pray. Talk about awkward and embarrassing? Once I did it I felt the burden of it lift right then. Then I asked God why He wanted me to do that and why me? Then, what God allowed me to find out next is nothing short of amazing.

A couple of months went by; I found out that the guy I had prayed for had testicular cancer. He had it prior to my praying for him. What God later revealed to me was that his cancer was trying to return and because of my obedience to pray for him, the cancer was not going to come back. From my understanding he is living a healthy life and is blessed. I can't wait to see the miracle children that he will have because of God's healing and continual restoration.

My question now to God was why me? This was God's response: God knew that the gentleman would not believe nor allow anybody else but me to do so because of past dealings with religious folks and past hurts from the church. I represent something new, fresh and radical.

I would be willing to do anything at least once; even if that meant taking my -- sometimes arrogant, well-mannered, well-educated, conscience self -- to pray for another man's testicles and not suffer from a homophobic reaction and worry about the naysayers. I serve that kind of God -- a God that uses people to help people. Just think what if I did not be obedient? I don't know if I could live with myself knowing that I could have been used to change the outcome.

See, we must understand that being obedient is not always for you, but you may be saving somebody else. Now if I knew that the gentleman had suffered from a male specific form of cancer, then I probably would not have hesitated as much but I didn't. Who has God sent you to minister to and you hesitated because of self? I don't know how much time I had left to obey but I am glad I did and I encourage you to obey right away.

 Until tomorrow, if it's the Lord's will,

Gospel Professor

Day 37

Jesus said, "I am the Way, the Truth and the Light."

There is no other way, no other truth, and no other light.

What we are looking for we can find in Jesus.

Jesus said, "Let he that is greatest among you be a servant" *(Matthew 23:11)*. I am finding the taste of milk to be bitter and the taste of meat to be sweeter. I say that to say I am learning to be a real servant and I like it. Being a servant is not an easy task, but yet a rewarding one especially when you get to serve the King. A good servant in a restaurant can make a bad meal tolerable. My wife and I have been places where the food was not very good, however, the service was some of the best we ever had. The good service made my experience at the place better and made me want to give the place at least a second chance for my patronage. On the other hand I have been to restaurants with excellent food and the worst service of all time. So, I don't return to restaurants like this. In my opinion good food is everywhere, but good service isn't. This brings me to my point today.

Are you a good servant? **Being a good servant can take you a long way; it can make up for your lack of abilities.** People usually appreciate good service and are more tolerable of you. Good servants are hard to find. God looks at us much the same way. He is not worried about your shortcomings and your lack of abilities He just wants your best service -- whatever it is.

Many times I see people in the body of Christ that are discouraged because they don't have the gifts that others possess. They feel that what they have is not important and does not have a place in the house of the Lord. The reason you have the gifts and talents that God gave you is because He needs them from you and He gave you the ability to serve Him with them. You are somebody and the gifts that you have to serve with are important to us all. **Your service**

does not have to be recognized by a worldly authority to be seen as a heavenly gift.

I suffered a long time with finding my place in the service of God. I knew that I was a man of unique talent, but because my talents did not seem to fit what seemed to be the status quo of my religious affiliations, I felt that I did not matter. I almost aborted my ministry several times and thought to myself that if I was going to die and go to hell I should at least enjoy the trip. However, God's power and love would not allow me to do that. I struggled for years and often times things happened to remind me of that struggle.

See, where I was raised all of the men of God could sing, shout, have great oratorical skills and had a certain swagger about them. I don't have those talents; I can't carry a note at all, I can't dance, I am a rhythm-less nation, I talk fast, and I have a tendency to stutter at times.

Then God made me realize that I only had to please him;

that speaking and teaching His Word was not emotionalism, it was about changing lives. He made me look at what I could do and do well. I was bold -- not scared -- to speak my mind to anybody, tactfully of course. I realized that I was genuine and I really loved to help people, period. I was smart and strategic; He had given me the ability to think via the mathematical mind He had given me. I am a leader by design.

I have learned and embraced being radical. The way I see it you and I are Jesus' Project (www.daJesusProject.com). He is always working on us. My ministry *Finding Fish (Matthew 4:19)* is more evangelistic because Jesus told us to go find "them." He did not say they were going to jump in the boat. The t-shirts (www.dajesusproject.com/market) that I have on my website, it's about spreading the message on all platforms. The Youtube, Twitter, and Facebook sites have made me an international ministry without spending one cent. Lastly, the Apple pod cast has given me a

192

platform to spread the gospel for free without being the pastor of a church or receiving donations.

Now, if He can bless me to be able to do all of this and more without pastoring a congregation, I can only imagine what He can do with the help of a congregation. It would not surprise me if He is doing more with me this way than He could have done if He allowed me to be accepted by the religious institutions that would not consider me worthy enough to be one of them. But I would not trade it for my journey now.

Take what you have and move forward with it. Your gift will make room for you, because you are the only one who can serve the King in the unique way that He expects from you.

Until tomorrow, if it's the Lord's will,

Gospel Professor

Day 38

The Lord is my shepherd I do not want. Christ is the Good Shepherd, and none of His sheep have lack or need of anything. Where the Shepherd guides, He provides.

Day 38 of the 40 day fast is in the books and what a day it was. God always knows what you need and when you need it. If you have not figured it out by now I am an avid reader. I inherited that trait from my father. When I was younger, I always saw my father with a book of some sorts. As a child I picked up the love of reading and like most teenagers I lost the love at some point. When I became an adult, my love of pleasure reading returned. I typically do not read fiction, in my opinion it's a waste of time. I read a lot of religious, political, self-help commentary outside of the Bible. One of my favorite authors is Dr. Cornel West and I have had the pleasure of meeting him twice at the universities where I worked. I have been fortunate to meet many significant public figures in my short span on earth.

They each had an impact on me in different ways, and so

did Dr. West.

When I heard Dr. West, I was intrigued by some of the

things he said. He gave confirmation to the things that I had

talked about on day 37 of service. He gave words of

wisdom on the differences of success and greatness.

Success and greatness are issues that I have had a great

internal conflict with. Like anyone, I want both of them on

a high level. I often wonder what would happen if I had to

choose. What if I was destined to only have one of them?

What would I choose -- success or greatness? It's a difficult

choice. In some instances **I believe that you can earn**

success, but I also think that you are handpicked by

God for greatness. Yes anybody can be successful with a

good work ethic, good decisions, and a solid foundation.

However, to be great requires the ultimate sacrifice, to

achieve it. Yes all of the "greats" have it in common –

Jesus (Greatest of all time), Malcolm X, Martin Luther King, Abraham Lincoln, Cornel West, Mother Theresa, Gandhi, Martin Luther, TD Jakes, Barack Obama, my father, and many more. Got it yet?

They all gave of themselves in service to humanity for the better good. Some of them lived with the threat of their humanity being taken away and others have just given of themselves with relentless pursuit. To be great is a relentless pursuit to serve others and fight against the injustices in our society. Let me help put it into perspective what these individuals contributed to us.

Jesus is the Savior of the world, a friend to the poor, and a champion of love.

Malcolm X lost his life after he found out how to love all people.

Abraham Lincoln lost his life after realizing the he could help to end injustice.

Cornel West risks his life to talk unapologetically to people of all races about social injustice against the poor and

weak.

Mother Theresa spent her life serving the poor in India and

caring for the poor around the world.

Gandhi spent his life teaching peace and servant-hood for

all men and started the nonviolent protest movement.

Martin Luther King, Jr. served and lost his life being the

leader of the civil rights' movement by borrowing the

teaching of Gandhi in the form of nonviolent protest.

Martin Luther was a great theologian that stood against the

wrongs of his time when he took the bold stand to dispute

that punishment from sin could not be avoided by paying

money.

TD Jakes dares to go against the grain in that he follows the

ministry of Jesus Christ and meets people where they are

and encourages and shows them the way out through the

cross.

Barack Obama endures constant threats and scrutiny of his

life as he leads a country where some younger generations embrace the progress, while some older generations are in denial of the hate and bigotry that still exist in their hearts. My father, who made our dreams his dreams and gave up his own dreams to endure the mockery of others that doubted his ways of discipline and investigative approaches to teaching his children.

God never ceases to amaze me. Just as I was writing today I had a friend of mine call. We have not talked in a while but God used him to confirm that service is truly great. He went on to tell me that he and his wife were following my fast from afar and how God was working through his life. Wow, you have to trust me when I tell you that this is a blessing to see how far God has brought this man and he is not finish yet. It's in you to serve -- just do it.

Two nuggets I want to share before I shut up for today. I picked these up from Dr. West when I listened to him at a recent campus lecture. The first one is that, "Justice **is love**

shown publicly" Think about the ministry of Jesus and all of the justice He brought throughout His life. The other Dr. West talked about was this notion called, "finding your voice". This notion struck me, because this whole fast was about me essentially finding my voice. I can see more clearly that my voice is to be candid and honest, to break the box of religion and to help people where they are. It may be through books, blogs, t-shirts, websites, or personal conversations.

During this fast I feel like I have had a coming out party, or a record release of who I am. People have been calling me, writing and communicating in many various forms. It's all for service to the Kingdom of God, for no monetary gain (except maybe from the sale of this book you are reading).

And one more thing... I just remembered a prophecy that I received about nine months ago that I was a fisherman (those of you that know me personally know that I am) and that I had a hook that would catch fish without bait.

I am excited because I believe this is what God is doing in my life right now – hook, line and sinker.

Now keep working until you find your voice!

Until tomorrow, if it's the Lord's will,

Gospel Professor

Day 39

Almost there day 39 of the 40-day fast was pretty much smooth sailing. I've done a lot of thinking about various things today. Do you ever take the time out just to think? I think you would be surprised what things -- both good and bad -- you come up with. I am a firm believer that **everything that we are ever going to be is within is**. In some of us it's buried under junk. In some of us it's closer to the top, and others already know what it is but are digging deeper to reveal more. Which one are you?

Is your life so cluttered with stuff that you cannot do the things that you know you should do? I will be the first to admit that I at various times have been caught up in the rat race of life. Then, I realized that I might be working toward something that is unobtainable. Dr. Cornel West said something in lecture that got me to thinking. He said, "We all have to find our own pace in this life. You can't sprint the entire way because it's a marathon".

This fast for me has been about realizing the things God has put in me and teaching me how to properly use them. I realized that the things that I was "sprinting" to obtain from others were already inside of me, but I did not take the time to look. Yes, I have to give props to my grandfather Bishop Johnnie Alston, as much as I hate to admit it, he was right. He used to tell me that I better get some patience or God has a way of taking you through things for you to get it. I usually pride myself on being a quick learner, but this was not a lesson that came quickly for me. It has been the hardest lesson I have ever learned. But I think I got it now. **You have to run the race at a pace where you can keep up.**

Yes, I started this race at a record pace -- Usain Bolt would not have given me a run for my money. I was running fast to get there and I was not sure where *there* was. So when I got there I did not know it and I did not enjoy the scenery on the way. They say that it's lonely at the top for a few reasons:

The air is thin up there -- everyone will not have the lungs to breathe when they get there because you have to train for it, and experience some hardships or feeling like you're going to die and learn to make the best out of your limited resources to be able to dwell and breathe there.

Everybody does not aspire to be there -- some just don't have the discipline to do what it takes to get there. The fasting, the praying, the studying, the character, the sacrifice, the ridicule, etc., I think you get it. These types of things keep many by the wayside.

The silent war -- the self-battle that we are fighting everyday. God's plan and the talents that

He has given me only limit what I can do. I figured out that I worked hard for years for something that God never meant for me to have. That equals wasted time, energy, and effort. I wasted this time because I did not know what God's plan was for me and I followed the paths that seemed right to me. Now if I had focused all of this time and energy into the will of God I would have avoided the many pitfalls and frustrations that I have encountered. Finally, I understand it now!

Therefore, I have found my stride, and I have a pace that helps me to finish the race. **I run the race according to the plan He has set for me.** I can clearly see the map and the course I have to take. I no longer have to be frustrated because I can see that all of these things working together for my good. When my enemy raises his hand against me, I remember reading on the map that, "No weapon formed against me will prosper." When I am running and I get thirsty, I am reminded that, "I can get water from the rock."

When I start to slow my pace a little I see an eagle over head and I recall that, "They that wait upon the Lord shall renew thy strength. They shall mount up like wings of an eagle, they shall run and not be weary they shall walk and not faint." When I start to see people pass me in the race because it seems that my pace is slow, I hear a voice telling me that, "The race is not given to the swift or to the strong but to the one that endures to the end." When I get to the finish line I want to be like Paul and say I ran the race, I have finished my course and I have fought a good fight (2 Timothy 4:7). Then I look forward to those words: "Well done, thy good and faithful servant. Well Done." (Matthew 25:23).

Until tomorrow, if it's the Lord's will,

Gospel Professor

Day 40

This is it! Day 40 of the 40-day fast. It's hard to believe but the fast is over today. While hunting today I did a lot of thinking about this fast. This fast has certainly changed me, but how? There are many things that come to mind when I look back over the last 40 days of my life. There has been some changing, introspection and growth in all aspects of my life. Change is needed in our life to help us propel to our next level or destiny in life. Life is like a pond that does not receive fresh water. A pond that does not receive fresh water gains harmful bacteria and usually stunts the growth of the fish in that water. It is the perfect habitat for mosquitoes and other parasites. Usually nothing good comes from stagnant water. However, like the pools of Bethesda in the Bible, the waters need to be troubled (John 5:4). The troubling of the water brings about change; it kills those harmful things that were growing in your life.

During this birthing process I have learned patience. Patience was a tough lesson for me to learn. I realized how anxious I was to do things and make stuff happen. As I thought more I realized that the things that I was anxious for were things that I did not have control over. If I have not learned anything else during this fast, I have learned that **I cannot control anything. God is totally in control** and I just react to the various situations that He allows me to be in. I really understand that how I react to a situation really determines what happens next.

Being at the end of this process I have also realized that the birthing process has been the easy part compared to that which is to come. Taking the things that I have given birth to and feeding them properly will take even more effort. It's one thing to have a baby, but it's another thing to take care of one and meet all of its needs until it's able to meet the needs on its own.

We put all of our energy into the birthing process without the thought of what it will take to keep the birth alive. Look at it from a natural point of view: Take for example a woman that is pregnant, she stays pregnant for nine months and gives birth to a person that will live on average about seventy years. **The thing that is birthed has the potential to be around much longer than the process to get it there.**

So yes, the fast was very tough at times but this short period of trial and self-discipline gives me something that will live for a lifetime.

I may never do this again, nonetheless, it was truly worth every meal missed, every decision made, and everything revealed. I can now say without a doubt that I have spent time with the King and have His seal.

Until tomorrow, if it's the Lord's will,

Gospel Professor

6 Months Later

CONCLUSION

Conclusion

Fasting is a life altering experience. From what you have read you can clearly see that my life has changed. I have grown tremendously in my spiritual walk with the Lord, and I have gotten significantly smaller physically as well. ***This 40-day fasting process was me growing from milk to the meat things of God.*** When you are on milk you are not as strong; you need to be protected, nurtured, and cared for. At some point during your walk with Christ you have to become weaned off the milk and start to chew on some of the meaty things of this walk.

The more you go through and conquer, your faith is increased and you are ready to face tougher tasks, this is growth. Growth is not always seen in large quantities but consistent growth will be equated to large growth in time.

I have come out of this fast being more patient with God and His plan. Knowing that He has a path set for me, and I have to choose to follow it. It is a mindset change. The Bible says, "When I was a child I thought as a child, I spoke as a child. But when I became a man I put away childish things" (1 Corinthians 13:11). Growth causes you to look at the world and your Christian walk very differently. When you develop an unshakeable confidence in God and who He is, you may have once seen the glass as being half empty, but you now see it as being half full. You understand only to do things that you are anointed by God to do. You now have no problem telling others when you know something is outside of your gifting and you're calling to do. Growing up also causes you to examine your relationship with God and to know where you stand. I have learned all of these things while being on this fast.

The Fasting Chronicle has been a pleasure to share with you and I hope that it has been a blessing as well as an inspiration to your life. Don't forget to tell others about it. I will leave you with this last thing: Jesus loved us unconditionally so remember this, "You can't serve the people, if you don't love the people. Love everybody and yourself."

Until next time,

Gospel Professor.

Day 1 of 40 day fast

Day 21 of 40 day fast

Day 42 of 40 day fast

Da Jesus Project Publishing

Coming Soon

Dorothy "aW" Williams

Angel Writer

www.daJesusProject.com

or

publishing@dajesusproject.com

Notes

www.ingramcontent.com/pod-product-compliance
Lightning Source LLC
Chambersburg PA
CBHW032116040426
42449CB00005B/166